KS3 ICT Workbook

To accompany our KS3 ICT Study Guide we've produced this marvellous Workbook. It's packed with useful questions to make sure that you can tackle KS3 ICT with confidence.

It's also, well, kinda entertaining, if we do say so ourselves. Quite an achievement for an ICT workbook, really...

Contents

SECTION ONE — THE PARTS OF A COMPUTER SYSTEM

Data 1

Computer Systems 2

Computerised vs. Manual Systems 3

Computer Security 4

Input Devices 5

SECTION TWO — USING A COMPUTER SYSTEM

Data Capture 7

Data Capture — Form Design 8

Benefits and Problems of Data Collection 9

Data Storage and Processing 10

Data Presentation 11

SECTION THREE — SYSTEMS ANALYSIS

Step One — Identifying the Problem 12

Analysis — The Feasibility Study 13

Design — Input, Process, Output 14

Flow Diagrams 15

Writing a Procedure 16

SECTION FOUR — TEXT AND IMAGE PROCESSING SOFTWARE

Word Processing Basics 17

Word Processing — Advanced Features 19

Creating Images 21

Graphics — Changing Images 22

Editing Digital Images 23

Desktop Publishing — Basics 24

Working with Frames 25

Producing a Newspaper 26

Presentation Software 27

SECTION FIVE — SPREADSHEETS AND DATABASES

Spreadsheets — The Basics 29

Spreadsheets — Simple Formulas 30

Spreadsheets — Charts and Graphs 31

Spreadsheet Models and Simulations 32

Databases 33

SECTION SIX — THE INTERNET

Internet Basics 37

Researching a Topic 38

Searching for Information 39

Fact and Opinion 41

Designing a Web Page 42

Creating a Web Page 43

Creating a Web Page — The Harder Bits 44

Designing a Website 45

E-Mail 46

Address Books 47

SECTION SEVEN — COMPUTERS IN THE REAL WORLD

Computers in Shops 48

More Computer Applications 49

Even More Computer Applications 50

Measurement — Data Logging 51

Logging Period and Logging Interval 52

Measuring Physical Data 53

Computers and the Law 54

Computers and the Workplace 55

Computer Use — Health and Safety Issues 56

Published by Coordination Group Publications Ltd.

Contributors:
Mike Davis
Colin Harber Stuart
Chrissy Williams
Simon Little
Victoria Brereton
Alice Shepperson
Dominic Hall
James Paul Wallis

ISBN: 1 84146 292 6

Groovy website: www.cgpbooks.co.uk

Jolly bits of clipart from CorelDRAW

Printed by Elanders Hindson, Newcastle upon Tyne.

Section One — The Parts of a Computer System

Data

Q1   Copy and complete each of the following sentences, using the words on the pig:

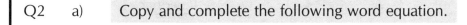

   a)   Computers run on ....

   b)   Computers are made up of a number of electric ....

   c)   Each circuit within a computer can either be ....

   d)   Computers use a .... code that consists of only .... digits.

   e)   A circuit that's switched .... represents the digit 1
        and a circuit that's switched .... represents the digit 0.

Q2   a)   Copy and complete the following word equation.

   Information = ... + Meaning

   b)   Copy out the table to the right and indicate
        which of the statements are data and
        which are information by placing
        an 'X' in the appropriate column.

Statement	Information	Data
My birthday is 11071988		
01539 77 88 99		
CR 15 07 13Z		
Miss Johnson is 35		
Your balance is £666		

Q3   Read the sentences below and decide which are true and which are false.
   Copy out the statements that are true.

   a)   Computers are machines that process data.

   b)   Computers are clever; they understand the data that they process.

   c)   If you get a computer to process data that is incorrect, the results will be meaningless.

   d)   GIGO stands for Grab It Get Out.

   e)   Data is information that has no meaning without a context.

Q4   *Asif wishes to back-up some important computer data.*
   His computer copies files at a speed of 1 million bytes per second.

   How long (in seconds) will it take to copy each of the following:
   (Use the hints on the cows.)

   a)   One letter (20Kb)

   b)   One hundred tunes (5Gb in total)

   c)   Thirty digital pictures (1Mb in total)

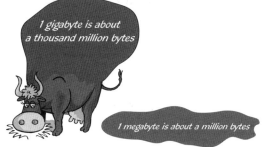

Computer Systems

Q1   A computer system can be broken down into 3 simple parts
    — input, process and output. Say which part each of these falls into:

.   a)   Print out results.   d)   Display results on the screen.

    b)   Validate data.   e)   Convert information to data.

    c)   Turn input data into something else.   f)   Verify data.

Q2   *The diagram below is a simple representation of the flow of data in a computer system.*

    a)   Copy the diagram below and complete the labelling using the words on the right.

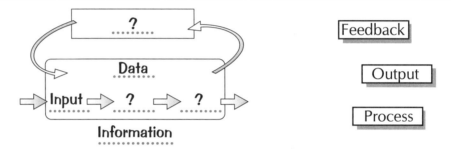

    b)   Say which of the following is the correct name
    for the part of the computer that does the processing.

        i) Calculator   ii)   Central Processing Unit (CPU)   iii)   Abacus

Q3   *Harriet is helping her ICT teacher to design a computerised register. She has been given the
task of ensuring that the data that is entered is validated by the system.*

    Match each piece of data to the correct validation check.

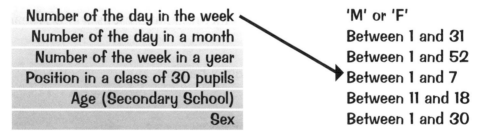

Q4   *Rayna uses her father's computer to record and process the results of her hockey team.*

    Copy the following sentences, then state whether the activity takes place
in the Input, Data Processing or Output part of the computer system.

    a)   Teams are ranked according to their points score.

    b)   Rayna checks that she has entered the scores correctly.

    c)   Final positions can be viewed on the screen.

    d)   The last round of results are typed into the computer.

    e)   Rayna sends a printed copy of the league table to each of her team mates.

    f)   Teams are allocated 3 points for a win, 1 point for a draw and 0 points for a loss.

Computerised vs. Manual Systems

Q1   What type of software would the government use to store
information about all the cars registered in the UK?

A   Wordprocessor

B   Database

C   Anti-virus

Q2   Say which of the following is NOT a benefit of using a computerised system.

a)   Searching for records is very quick

b)   More than one person can access the data

c)   More people are needed to operate the computer system than a paper based system

Q3   Copy and complete the following sentences using the words in the axe:

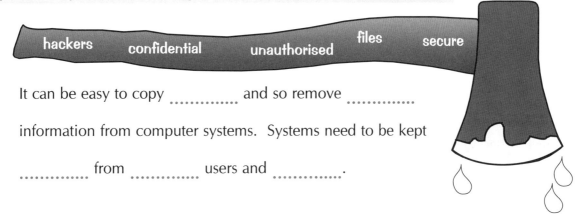

hackers   confidential   unauthorised   files   secure

It can be easy to copy .... and so remove ....

information from computer systems. Systems need to be kept

.... from .... users and ....

Q4   *Teachers at Thrasham High School write all their end of year reports for pupils by hand.*

Write down two disadvantages of writing the reports by hand
over using a computerised system.

Q5   *Sally Jones runs a doctors' surgery. She is thinking of introducing
a computer system. It will replace the existing paper based system.
The system will be used by all the staff who work at the surgery.*

Write down three potential problems of introducing the computer system.

Q6   *Mr Eriksson is a busy builder who manages a local football club with 100 members.*

Give three reasons why he should computerise his records.

Computer Security

Q1 There are three types of computer security.
Unjumble the words below into a sentence about each one.

A   protects Physical the hardware. security

B   security the network. limits use of Access

C   Data data. loss security prevents of

Q2 Copy and complete the sentence below by using the words in the box to fill in the blanks.

| users | network | passwords | names | controlled |

Access to a .... is .... by giving all authorised ....

user .... and asking them to create their own ....

Q3 *Nicholas has set up his ICT pupils as authorised users and given them user names.*
Each of them has chosen a password.

What will he advise them to do with their password frequently?

Q4 *Carole's dad's computer was badly damaged during a fire at his factory.*
Although he had to buy a replacement computer, he was still able to access all his data.

Give two precautions that he must have taken to make this possible.

Q5 *You have just been appointed ICT Manager at your local school.*

a)   Write down three things that you would do to
adequately protect your hardware from theft.

b)   Explain two measures that you might take to minimise damage in case of fire.

Q6 *Justine Front has bought herself a new computer. Justine is worried that the computer might get*
stolen. She wants to do something to make sure it's identifiable as her computer.

Write down two things that Justine should write on the computer
to help the police to identify the computer.

Fishermen get insecure about their net work too...
Security only works if you use it properly. A password is only any good if you keep it secret —
don't choose something obvious, don't tell anyone what it is ...and don't write it on your face in felt tip.

Input Devices

Q1   Copy and complete the following sentence, using two words:

Hardware which is used to enter data into the computer is called an ....

Q2   Copy out the list below and say whether each one
        is a feature of a QWERTY or CONCEPT keyboard.

Alpha-numeric keys

Picture keys

The most common input device

Used in fast food restaurants

Limited use

Very fast to use

Multi use

Similar information entered over and over

Used with office and home computers

looks a bit
qwerty to me...

Q3   Say which of the following statements are true and which are false:

a)   A computer mouse has bigger teeth than a real mouse.

b)   Mouse buttons can be clicked or double clicked to give the computer a command.

c)   Under the mouse is a mirror.

d)   All computer mice are called Jerry.

e)   A ball under the mouse rotates when the mouse is moved over a flat surface.

f)   A mouse is used to move the cursor on the screen.

Q4   Name two devices that can be used instead of a mouse, e.g. with a laptop.

Q5   What input device lets you draw pictures directly into
        a computer as if you were using a pen and paper?

Raymond likes kittens — he's a man not a mouse...

Three fine mice, three fine mice, see how they move the cursor, see how they move the cursor...
Look how easy it is to write fun rhymes about ICT... Yes, there's no limit to the fun of learning ICT.

Input Devices

Q1 Choose words from the lists below to write 6 sentences that follow this structure:
'A *INPUT DEVICE* is used to enter *DATA TYPE* into the computer'.

INPUT DEVICE
Scanner, Keyboard, Digital Camera,
Laser Scanner, Microphone, Sensor.

DATA TYPE
Photographic Images, Printed Images,
Bar Codes, Text, Sound, Environmental data.

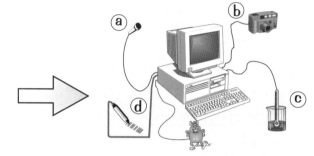

Q2 Identify each of the input devices in the
diagram to the right (ignore the mouse).

Q3 *Boris is a salesperson for LASCAN Data Capture Systems.*
He is trying to sell a laser-scanning system to the owner of a small supermarket. Currently the
supermarket puts price tags on each item and the price of each item is typed into the cash till.

a) In your own words explain what the laser scanners are used for.

b) State two benefits that Boris should tell the manager about.

c) Write down two problems that the manager might mention to counter Boris' claims.

Q4 Use the words in Doody's mouth to complete these sentences about digital cameras.

a) Digital cameras save an image
as a series of dots called ....

b) The image from a digital camera can be ....
to a computer and edited
using .... – .... software.

c) Photographic .... is not needed and
the .... is available for immediate use.

d) A digital image can be sent as an
.... attachment to anywhere in the world.

e) High resolution images use lots of ....
and also lots of .... power.

pixels film
memory
battery
photo-editing
e-mail image
uploaded

Q5 Credit cards have a short length of magnetic tape on the back.
Name three pieces of information stored on it.

Data Capture

Q1 Explain how a gas company might use a semi-automatic turnaround document system to record customers' readings without having to visit their premises.

Q2 Copy and complete each of the following sentences using the words from the box.

two-part	data	key	hand
capture	sensors	scanners	

a) Gathering information to put on a computer system is called ..... capture.

b) Data collection is a ..... - ..... process.

c) Questionnaires usually need someone to ..... in the results by ..... .

d) Automatic data ..... means collecting information from ..... and ..... .

Q3 a) Explain the difference between manual and automatic data capture.

b) Copy the following table and use it to explain the advantages and disadvantages of each type of data capture mentioned.

Example	Advantages	Disadvantages
Questionnaire		
Temperature sensor		
Bar-code reader		
Multiple choice exam answer sheet (where answers are read by machine)		

Q4 *Claire and Tim are spending their summer holidays working for the local council. A new traffic system has been put in place and the council is keen to see how effective it is.*

a) *Claire has been asked to find out the views of the public.*

Explain how she would go about her task. What method of data capture would she use and how would the data be transferred to the computer?

b) *Tim, on the other hand, is to use equipment provided by the council to monitor traffic flows.*

State **two** reasons why this data must be captured automatically.

Q5 *Fabien has been asked by his Bandito boss to find out if a number of families enjoyed a recent Bandito fireworks display. He has written a questionnaire but, as there were over 200 people at the bonfire, he would like to use his boss's computer system and scanner to speed the job up.*

Re-design Fabien's questionnaire into a data-capture form that will allow the answers to be read by a scanner.

> Questionnaire:
> What type of fireworks did you like best?
> Was the bonfire hot enough?
> Were the gangsters scary enough?

Data Capture — Form Design

Q1 Copy and complete the following sentences using the words on the reindeer.

a) Forms that .... data must be well ....

b) If the form is not filled in .... the .... will be ....

designed
properly
capture
data
useless

Q2 *Julia runs a riding school in the Merekent valley. She is creating a database of information about her pupils. Her form, which is not well designed, is shown below.*

> Merekent Riding Academy
> Please fill in this form and send it back to me.
> Personal details.
> When do you ride?
> Which horses?

Re-design the form so that she gets the information she needs.

Q3 *Myra is in charge of the school library recorded music collection. Students often need to reserve the CD or tape that they want as there is only one copy of each.*

Design and draw a form that will ensure that she can input the following data into the library's computer.

a) Title of album.

b) Artist.

c) Date required.

d) Type of media — CD, tape, minidisk.

e) Details of person making reservation, including contact number.

Q4 *Frank has designed the form on the right to help him plan his courses for the leisure centre. He wants to find out what activities the centre users enjoy most. He intends to leave the forms with Reception. He shows the form to his manager, Paula.*

a) Write down **five** improvements that Paula might suggest.

b) Re-draw the form to take account of the comments.

> What do you do at the Leisure Centre?
> How long do you stay?
> How often do you come to the centre?
> When do you usually come?
> What would you like to do?
> Personal details:
> Give this form in when you leave.

Benefits and Problems of Data Collection

Q1 Say which of the following are the **three** main ways that you can lose data if it is stored on a computer.

PC getting a bit depressed after it's been dumped for a laptop

Hackers

Corrupt files

Corrupt politicians

Hecklers

Damage to hardware

Q2 Using your own words, explain:

a) what a computer virus is, and what it does.

b) how data can be lost through hardware failure.

c) what a hacker can do to a computer system.

Q3 *The table below should show the advantages and disadvantages of computer data storage. But it's all muddled up, like my mate Andy.*

Re-write the table with each point under the correct heading.

Advantages.	Disadvantages.
Quick and easy to search for records.	Takes up less space than filing cabinets.
Confidential files can be read or copied more easily.	Data is not completely safe.
	Expensive to set up.
Staff need to be trained to use the system.	Easier to produce reports and analyse data.
Fewer staff needed.	More than one person can look at the data at the same time.

Q4 *The 'Spirit of the Lakes' is a small hotel situated in a remote part of Cumbria. It has neither mains water nor mains electricity. It stocks over 100 different varieties of beers and spirits. The owner keeps a record of each product on a stock card in his office. This information needs to be read by his wife, the hotel staff and his cellar manager.*

a) Suggest **four** advantages to the hotel of storing this information on a computer system.

b) Bearing in mind his location, describe two possible ways that his data could be lost.

I've got a hacking cough — heeuEeeUuGHHh hg ugh...

Some questions are easier than they look. If you're getting stuck on Q3, take a deep breath and look at the bits, one at a time. You only need to work out if each one's a <u>good thing</u> or a <u>bad thing</u>.

Data Storage and Processing

Q1 A data file is organised into records and fields. For each of the
following, say whether it would be a data file, a record or a field:

a) Address Book.

b) Personal details of an individual.

c) Address.

d) Telephone number.

Q2 Say whether each of the following sentences is true or false:

a) Fixed length fields have a fixed number of characters.

b) Variable length fields are quicker to process.

c) Fixed length fields use less memory.

d) A variable length field is only as long as it needs to be.

Q3 a) There are two important ways that computers can process data.
Pick them out from the words below.

Real-time   Meal-time   Batch   Gareth Gates

Acely   Beware the dark side

b) A cinema ticket booking and a wage calculation are examples of these different types
of processing. Say which is which, and explain how they are processed differently.

Q4 *Mintcake Ltd keep data about their staff on a computer which they use to calculate their wages.*

a) Explain how personnel data could be split into records and fields.

b) Copy out the types of data below and write down what type of field
(fixed-length or variable-length) you would use for it:

Worker's name   Date of Birth   Address   Post Code.

Q5 *Rocky is a pedigree Lakeland Terrier. His details are kept on the Kennel Club's computer.
Once a month, his owners receive a newsletter informing them about dog shows, puppies etc.*

a) What type of processing does the Kennel Club use to send out the newsletter?

b) What type of processing do they use to add a new dog to the system?

The sun is warming my PC's heart — whatta daytafile...

All this processing malarky seems a bit annoying to me. Quite repetitive. Well that's data files for
you. Still, it's all stuff you <u>have</u> to know, and once you <u>do</u> know it, the days will just fly by. Ahh...

Data Presentation

Q1   Below are six ways in which information can be presented. The list has become corrupted, resulting in letters changing into Jumbo Wilson photos. Write down what each word should be.

    T◼◼T   ◼OU◼D   PICT◼◼◼S   G◼A◼◼S A◼D C◼ARTS   MU◼◼IME◼IA

Q2   Copy and complete the table using the list of positive points in the box.

	Screen Display	Hard Copy
Pros		

> Information can be edited immediately.
> Multimedia presentations are possible.
> Permanent record.
> Can be viewed without a computer.
> Sound and moving images.

Q3   Write down the disadvantages of using the following ways to present information:

    a)   Sound   b)   Text   c)   Pictures

Q4   Copy and complete each of the following statements using words from the snails' backs:

    a)   Graphs show the .... between two or more sets of numbers.

    b)   Graphs can accurately .... complex information.

    c)   Charts are any image that communicates .... or .... information.

    d)   The reader of a chart or graph may need some mathematical .... to understand it.

 relationship   summarise   skill   logical   numerical

Q5   *Manuel was in charge of the very successful Spanish exchange to Barcelona. Students took digital pictures while they were there. They also recorded the locals speaking and playing traditional music. Manuel is preparing a presentation to the parents of the pupils.*

    a)   Suggest **four** different mediums that he could use to present his information.

    b)   Suggest **two** output methods that he could use to make his presentation better.

Q6   *Siobhan is the drummer for a local monkey band. She has lots of computerised information about her band including pictures, details of prizes won, growth of numbers of members, sound clips and press cuttings. She has approached a local firm for sponsorship and has to give a presentation to the board.*

    a)   Explain the advantages to her of using the following presentation methods:

       i)   Text   ii)   Graphs   iii)   Sound   iv)   Pictures

    b)   What should she do in case the firm do not have computer access in the boardroom?

Step One — Identify the Problem

Q1 For each of the following statements, say if it's true or false.

a) Systems analysis is the way that old information systems are turned into new information systems.

b) Systems analysis usually involves removing expensive computers and replacing them with a cheaper manual system.

c) Systems analysis is what the computer does when it decides how to execute a command.

Q2 Copy and complete the following system life cycle diagram using the phrases in the box.

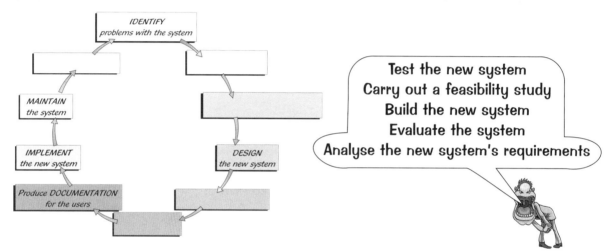

Q3 Copy and complete the following sentence, using your own words.

The systems life cycle is called a cycle because....

Q4 In your experience, are systems analysts normally:

a) cute, cuddly, hairy and called Barnaby?

b) the person who tries to understand the present system and its problems?

c) crazy as a dung beetle that thinks it's a pigeon?

Q5 *Hala Mistry is a systems analyst. She has been asked to identify the problems caused by the existing computer system in a medical centre.*

Write a paragraph to describe the various methods that Hala could use to find out what the problems are.

Analysis — The Feasibility Study

Q1 Which of the following is the correct definition of a feasibility study?

   a)   A feasibility study is when it is decided whether or not to use a systems analyst.

   b)   A feasibility study is where the requirements of the new system
        are analysed to help decide if the new system is worth creating.

   c)   A feasibility study is when it is decided if certain items of food
        should be stored in a fridge or freezer.

I can't live, if living is without you...

Q2 Copy and complete the following sentence using your own words.

> It is a good idea to set objectives for the new system because...

Q3 Say whether each of the following sentences about the rules
and constraints of a computer system is true or false.

   a)   The rules of the system are how various factors or constraints
        affect how the system operates.

   b)   Money is not a constraint on how large the computer system can be.

   c)   The computer system will have to operate within health and safety rules.

Q4 Copy and complete the following sentences using words from the box below.

feasibility	hardware	evaluation	computerised
ingenuity	design	changed	reversed
construction	pulverised	decisions	

As part of the .... study, the systems analyst needs to make .... about the

types of .... and software that will be used in the new system. These choices might

be .... later on, when he moves onto the .... stage of the system life cycle.

Q5 *Naz works for a mail order rollerblade business. He has a computer system which
takes five hours to produce a list of all the orders sent to customers in the previous month.
Naz would like to introduce a new system which only takes three hours to produce the
information.*

Write down an objective for the new system.

Staying awake for study — it's just not feasible...

This stuff could bore the hind legs off a dinosaur. And they had big legs. Just wait for that glorious
day when you'll be bigger than a dinosaur. And you'll crush ICT books like flies. Mwa-ha-ha-ha...

Design — Input, Process, Output

Q1 Which of the following is a benefit of using the code 'M'
when inputting the information 'Male' onto a computer?

    a)   It is easier for the user to understand what 'M' means.

    b)   The computer needs less memory to store 'M' than it needs to store 'Male'.

    c)   The computer won't auto-correct the word 'Male' to 'Mail'.

    d)   The computer won't get defensive.

Q2 Copy and complete the following sentences, using the words in the box.

The tasks that the .... needs to perform should be based on the original problems and
.... Code and commands will need to be written for each task — these might include
spreadsheet .... , database .... and word processing .... routines. Some
commands might involve .... data between different applications.

> exchanging   objectives   mail-merge   searches   formulas   system

Q3 *Boris Healey is designing a spreadsheet that will convert the results of a test
into percentages. The highest mark possible on the test is 60.*

Write down an example of each of the following types of test data:

    a)   Typical data   b)   Extreme data   c)   Invalid data

Q4 *Django Reinhardt is designing a database for a Fantasy Football League competition.
One item of data will be the position of a player in their team.*

The data will be one of the following:

goalkeeper, left sided defender, right sided defender, central defender,
left midfield, right midfield, centre midfield, forward

Suggest a suitable code that Django could use for each item of data.

Q5 Copy and complete the following sentences, using words in the box.

It is important for the output of a system to be ....
Users should only be shown the .... that they need.
It should be laid out in a format that they can ....
The layout of .... and printouts should first be
.... in rough. The rough sketches should then be
shown to the .... to check they are alright.

> understand   in code   users
> modelled   numbered   user-friendly
> output screens   processing screens
> commands   sketched   information

Flow Diagrams

Q1 Match the right name in the duck's mind to each of the following descriptions:

a) looks at the whole system by breaking down the main tasks into smaller tasks

b) describes the order in which the tasks of the system happen

Q2 Say whether the following sentences are true or false:

a) Top-down diagrams show what has to happen, not how they will happen.

b) Top-down diagrams are read from right to left.

Q3 Copy the following flow chart symbols and say what each one represents.

a) _(parallelogram)_   b) _(diamond)_   c) _(rectangle)_

Q4 *A doctors' surgery stores information about its patients on a computer database. The surgery wishes to add a new patient to the database and then print a copy of the patient's details.*

Draw a system flow chart to show how the computer system will do this.

Q5 *Doris Preston is a very lazy systems analyst. She is designing a system for a school. The school will collect information about each new pupil by asking parents to complete a form. Data from the form will be entered onto the school's computer database by hand. Finally, a copy of the information will be printed and given to the parent to check. Doris has completed the top half of the top-down diagram. She wants you to complete the bottom half. Because she's lazy.*

Copy and complete the diagram using the words to the right.

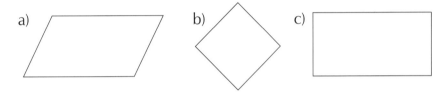
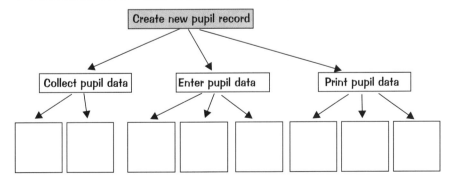

Words to use:
- Parent completes data capture form
- Print record
- Enter new pupil data
- Load pupil database
- Create new pupil record
- Check print preview
- Check printer for paper
- Give parent data capture form

Flow, flow, flow the chart gently down the page...

...merrily, merrily, merrily, merrily, ICT is such a rage. Flow charts and top-down diagrams are both useful ways of breaking down complex systems. Make sure you know the difference between them.

Writing a Procedure

Q1   Use one sentence to describe what a procedure is.

Q2   Choose the correct word from each pair below to describe an automatic car park ticket system.

a)   When you take a ticket, the car park entry barrier will (**raise** / **lower**).

b)   When a car passes over a (**pressure** / **temperature**) sensor,
an instruction is given to raise the exit barrier.

c)   When the entry barrier is raised, the computer counter total (**increases** / **decreases**) by 1.
When the exit barrier is raised, the counter total (**increases** / **decreases**) by 1.

d)   When the counter total equals the capacity of the car park,
the (**entrance** / **exit**) barrier is disabled.

Q3   Copy the following blank flow chart, filling in the blanks
for a car park **entry barrier** procedure.

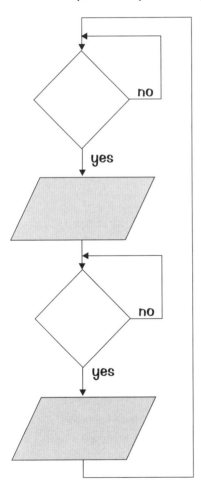

Q4   Explain why is it important to build big programs
out of small, simpler procedures.

Q5   _Bevan Morrison is responsible for the computer
system at a telephone mail order goat food
company. Bevan has set the following objectives
for his new computer system:_

"It must be able to store the records of
50,000 customers.

It must take less than 30 seconds to
enter the records of a new customer."

Bevan has evaluated his new system. He has
produced the following information:

"We currently have 48,000 customers.
We are adding 200 new customers
each week.

It currently takes 40 seconds to enter
the records of a new customer."

a)   How well does the system meet its objectives?

b)   Explain what should Bevan do?

Word Processing Basics

Q1   Which of the following is NOT a correct way to highlight a word?

    a)   Double click on the word

    b)   Hold down the SHIFT key while you move the text cursor using the cursor keys

    c)   Select EDIT and HIGHLIGHT WORD

Q2   Copy and complete the following sentences, using your own words:

    a)   The quickest way to highlight a paragraph of text is to...

    b)   Holding down the CTRL and SHIFT keys whilst moving the text cursor with the left or right cursor keys will...

Q3   Explain how the backspace key can be used for deleting text.

Q4   Explain what each of the following keyboard shortcuts does.

    a)   CTRL X

    b)   CTRL C

    c)   CTRL V

    d)   CTRL Z

Q5   *Doris Stoker has been asked by her boss to edit a letter that she created on her word processor last week. Her boss wants her to delete the sentence "We thank you for your recent order" and then replace it with the words "We are sorry to hear that you have cancelled your order."*

Describe two different ways that Doris could do this.

Q6   *Marco Blanc is a famous chef. He uses a word processor to enter and store his recipes. He wants to reorder several instructions in one of his recipes.*

Explain how Marco could use the word processor to rearrange the order of the instructions on the recipe.

Word Processing Basics

Q1   Copy and complete the following sentence using a word from the list below.

> The fancy name for the style of the letters in a document is ...

Feint	Font	Fount

Q2   Which of the following font sizes would be a suitable size for the main text in a normal word-processed document, e.g. a letter?

Aargh — the font — it's just too small...

a)   Size 6

b)   Size 12

c)   Size 18

Q3   *Look at the four examples of text below. Each one uses a different type of text-alignment.*

Copy and complete the table by writing the correct letter next to each type of alignment.

Alignment	Example
Left-alignment	
Right-alignment	
Centre-alignment	
Justified	

Q4   Copy and complete the following sentences using your own words.

a)   A benefit of using double-line spacing is...

b)   A drawback of using double-line spacing is...

Q5   *Ian Denting wants to write a letter to his favourite pop star. Ian wants to put his address at the top of the letter on the right hand side.*

Which type of indenting should Ian use to align his address?

Q6   *Luke Floorwalker is an ICT teacher at a large school. Luke wants to produce a poster of rules for using the school's computers. He wants the title "School Computer Rules" to stand out from the rest of the text.*

Describe THREE ways that Luke could change the appearance of this text to make it stand out.

Word Processing — Advanced Features

Q1 Copy and complete the following sentences. Use the words in the lovely picture.

Tables are a good way to present .... of .... information

e.g. lists of names and addresses. You can put ....

around tables, pictures or blocks of text. This helps to

.... the information on the page. .... can be created so

that the text flows down the page and .... to the next

column. This is good for ....

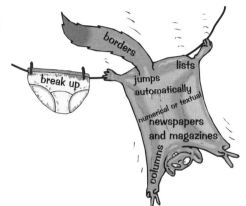

Q2 Pick out the correct word to complete each of these sentences.

a) The name for the information found at the top of a page is a (**corner** / **header**).

b) The name for the information found at the bottom of a page is a (**footer** / **throw-in**).

Q3 Say whether each of the following sentences about spell checkers is true or false.

a) A spell checker goes through your document
and picks up any words that aren't in its dictionary.

b) Spell checkers will find three types of error:
actual misspelt words, typing errors and missing words.

c) When the spell checker identifies a problem with a word
it will give you a list of alternative words.

d) You have to choose one of the alternative words suggested by the spell checker.

e) If you use a spell checker you will never need to proof read your work.

Q4 *Fred Needel has produced a twenty page school project using his word processor. Fred's teacher wants every page to contain the page number, date it was printed and the name of pupil.*

Explain how Fred could use his word processor to put this information onto every page.

Q5 Copy out the following paragraph. Correct the words which a spellchecker would identify as being misspelt. Underline the misspelt words which a spellchecker would not spot.

> In 1997 two men from Ipswich become the first men to land on Mars.
> Brian Jackson and Terry Smith blassted off in their home-made rocket and
> set out on a three weak jurney to the red plant. "Were amazed they
> managed to get their at all" said a neighbour. "Last time they tried to go to
> the moon they only got as far as Bury St Edmunds." "Mind you, nobody
> round here beleives them as they were seen later that day shoping in the
> local supermarcet."

Word Processing — Advanced Features

Q1 Copy and complete the following sentences using your own words.

    a)   The name for a standard document which contains the basic layout and formatting information is a ...

    b)   Two examples of uses for these documents are ...

Q2 Copy and complete the following sentences using the correct words around the chicken.

.... lets you send out .... letters by

combining a .... letter with ....

stored in a ....

Q3 Describe the stages involved in creating a mail merged letter.

Q4 Say whether each of the following sentences about importing information from other applications is true or false.

    a)   Importing means adding something created using a different software application.

    b)   An example is importing a clip art image into a word processed document.

    c)   Once the object has been imported it cannot be moved or resized.

    d)   You cannot import objects created using a spreadsheet into a word processed document.

Q5 *Mark Witherpen owns a video store in Millom. He wants to send a letter to all 327 customers in his database. The letter will tell each customer about the great new videos the shop has just added to its stock.*

Explain the benefits to Mark of using mail merge to create the letters.

why? why? oh why? I didn't ask for this...

Word Processing — I, why?...

Well, I have to say that mail merged letters are pretty cool. My mate Rhi was trying to raise money to go trekking in Indonesia, and she sent out letters like that to try and get money off people. Cool.

Creating Images

Q1   For each of the following, say which goat's sign ends the sentence correctly.

a)   Images made up of a series of coloured dots are called ...

b)   Images made up of separate lines and shapes are called ...

Q2   Say whether the following sentence is true or false.
If it's false, write down the correct version.

> Vector-based images usually require less memory than bitmap images.

Q3   Say whether each of the following sentences is true or false.

a)   A scanner can be used to create a vector-based image of a drawing or page in a book.

b)   The scanned image is made up of a series of pixels or dots.

c)   High resolution images contain a small number of pixels.

d)   Pictures saved using a digital camera are stored as JPEG files.

e)   JPEG files are bigger than bitmap files.

Q4   Which of the following is NOT a place where you can get clip-art from?

a)   CD-ROM

b)   Internet

c)   Digital camera

Q5   *Jason Darkley has been asked to design a new label for a can of sausages. He has found a good image of a sausage on the internet. He wants to use the image on the label.*

Explain why Jason might not be able to use the image.

Q6   *Sarah Weasel would like to include a photograph of her mother in her GCSE History project. Sarah is producing the project on her computer.*

Describe two ways that Sarah could put a photograph of her mother into the document.

Every picture paints 1000 words, or just one — Goats...

Sorry about the goats in this book. How many have there been so far — 2, 3, 4? Can't remember. Anyway, for this page, you've got to know your stuff. Don't guess the answers — look them up in a book and <u>learn them</u>.

Graphics — Changing Images

Q1 Copy and complete the following sentence using one of the words in the thought bubble.

> The process of changing the size of a graphic image is called....

resizing
morphing
reconfiguring

Q2 Look at the two images. Say what has been done to image A in order to end up with image B.

A  B

Q3 Say whether each of the following sentences about changing images is true or false.

a) An image can only be resized before it is imported into a desktop publishing package.

b) Only the edges of an image can be cropped.

c) Two or more images can be grouped together to make a new image.

d) Putting one image on top of another one is called grouping.

Q4 *Martha Midgeley wants to create an image of an angel sitting on top of a Christmas tree. Her clip art collection has pictures of angels and Christmas trees, but not in the same image.*

Explain how Martha could create her image.

Q5 *Jenny Baker wants to use an image of a frog to help her create a poster. Unfortunately the frog is too small.*

Explain how Jenny can make the frog bigger without squashing or stretching it.

Little house on the prairie dogs are cute...

Blimey — now this is what I call ICT. Drawing pictures and playing with prairie dogs. None of your spreadsheet nonsense. I tell you, I was born for this day and this day only. Woo-o...

Editing Digital Images

Q1 *You have scanned a copy of a colour photograph, but the image is too dark.*

Write down what you could do
to improve the quality of the image.

Q2 *You have taken a photograph using a digital camera, but the image is a little blurred.*

Write down what you could do to improve the quality of the image.

Q3 *You have taken a photo of a waterfall using a digital camera. You want to change the photo in a photo-editing program to make the image look like a watercolour painting.*

What kind of tool would you use to do this?

No matter how I paint,
it always looks like Clipart.

Q4 Copy and complete the following sentence, using a word from the box.

> If you change the hue value of an image you will change its ...

| **Size** |
| **Rotation** |
| **Colour** |

Q5 *Doris has a photo of her ex-boyfriend which she took with a digital camera. She wants to use photo-editing software to replace her ex-boyfriend's head with the head of a monkey.*

Explain in detail how she would do this.

How do monkeys make toast ? — put it under the g'rilla...

Arghhhggggrrghrhhh that was a terrible joke. Sorry. It's kind of cool to be able to do all this stuff to photos though. I'm quite impressed. Shame about Doris's bloke though. Looks like a stunner to me.

Desktop Publishing — Basics

Q1 Copy out the following table. Put a tick next to an item
if it is normally created using desktop publishing software.

Item	Created Using DTP?
Newspaper	
Poster	
Graphic image	
Customer database	
Pie chart	
Letter	
Leaflet	

Q2 Copy and complete the following sentences, using the words on the right.

DTP pages are built up as a series of .... For

example, ... frames contain text, and ....

frames contain images and so on. Frames can be

.... This means that it is very easy to ....

a DTP document by moving .... of text around.

Frames can also be moved from ....

Q3 a) What happens to the rest of the information
on the page when you delete an individual frame?

   b) What happens to the rest of the information when you
delete an object in a word processed document?

Q4 Say whether each of the following sentences is true or false.

   a) DTP often works best when source material is edited in other software
before being imported into the DTP program.

   b) The quality of a DTP document does not depend on the quality of the printer.

   c) It is easier to control the layout of a document using a word processor than using a DTP
program.

Q5 *Terry Osmond wants to produce a poster to advertise his new mobile fish and chip service.
He wants to use a word processor to create the poster.*

   Write down two reasons why Terry should use a DTP program to create the poster.

Q6 *Joan Osmond is the Deputy Headteacher at the Ozzy Osmond Secondary School.
She produces the school's end of term newsletter.*

   Explain how Joan could use DTP and other software to help her create the newsletter.

Working with Frames

Q1 Copy and complete the following sentence using a word from the box.

If you put a text frame on the left hand side of a page and another one on the right hand side you have created a document with two ...

attributes

columns

dimensions

Q2 Write down ONE benefit of linking two or more text frames together.

Q3 Write a sentence to explain what has been done to create the object below.

Bears bears bears bears bears
bears bears bears bears bears
bears bears bears bears bears
bears bears bears bears bears
bears bears bears bears bears
bears bears bears bears bears
bears bears bears bears bears
The weird thing about bears is
they get a really bad press when
actually they're   kinda cute
and they   don't smell
too bad.   Hey — why
are you   still reading?
Don't you know this is all nonsense?

Q4 Write down one benefit and one drawback of using templates to create DTP documents.

Q5 *Joan Osmond has now been promoted to Headteacher at the Ozzy Osmond Secondary School. She still has to produce the school's end of term newsletter because no one else will do it. Joan has asked you to help her to create a template for the newsletter.*

a) Write a list of the things that should be included in a template for the newsletter.

b) Draw a design sketch of the template.

Ozzy you never should have sold out...

These frame things can be quite tricky at first if you're used to using word processors. All you need is a bit of practice though, and you'll soon get the knack. Get on a computer and see...

Producing a Newspaper

Q1 Write down one benefit of using DTP to produce a newspaper.

Q2 Copy and complete the table by explaining what job each person does to help produce a newspaper.

Person	What They Do
Reporter	
Subeditor	
Photographer	
Editor	

Q3 Copy and complete these sentences, unjumbling the highlighted words.

a) The main part of a news article that contains the story is called the **yodb extt**.

b) The piece of text that contains information about the article, such as the name of the reporter and where the story was written is called the **by-lein**.

c) A short phrase designed to grab your attention and read the article is called the **neeladih**.

House your style?

d) A short sentence to briefly sum up what the story is about is called the **bigsunhead**.

e) The name for the lead story in a newspaper is the **shlaps**.

Q4 Say whether each of these is true or false.

a) A house style is the set of design and writing styles that the team producing the newspaper must follow.

b) The house style is chosen to reflect the skills of the people who produce the newspaper.

c) It includes things like advice on the fonts to be used and the writing style to be used.

d) It is up to each individual reporter to decide whether or not they use the house style.

Q5 *Gerry Bilder is the editor of the Millom Evening Star, the second biggest selling evening newspaper in the Millom area. Gerry is thinking of introducing a house style for the newspaper.*

Write down two benefits of the newspaper having a house style.

I just news you'd love this page...
Get out some papers and have a look at them. It's not hard and, if anyone asks, it's still revision. Wow, ICT gets me excited sometimes. It's a crazy rollercoaster of a subject isn't it?

Presentation Software

Q1 Write down ONE reason why a presentation might be given to an audience.

Q2 Copy and complete the following sentences about giving a presentation, using the words in the box.

The typical way to give a presentation is with a .... introducing the slides projected onto a .... The .... can read the information on the screen while the speaker gives them more detailed .... The other way is to give a presentation .... For this to work well, the slides have to be good enough to communicate all the required information by themselves. Multimedia presentation software can help by allowing a .... to be recorded.

> without a speaker   screen   commentary
>
> audience   spoken information   speaker

Tina thought it was about time she updated her software

Q3 Copy the following sentences about presentation software. For each sentence, say whether it is true or false.

a) Presentation software creates a series of slides in a single document.

b) Slides can contain either pictures or text, but not both on the same slide.

c) Pieces of information on a slide can be made to appear one at a time.

d) Animation effects can be used to make information arrive on a slide in interesting ways.

e) Animation effects can only be controlled by using a mouse or remote control button.

Q4 Write down three problems that might result from giving a presentation without using presentation software.

Q5 *Jemima Glossop has been asked to give a ten minute presentation on the topic of 'Carp fishing in Cumbria'. Jemima has decided to use presentation software to help create her slides.*

Describe THREE features of presentation software that Jemima could use to help improve the quality of her presentation.

Q6 *Martin Shore has produced a presentation to introduce a new software product to a group of teachers. He would like to adapt the presentation so that it can be put onto a website. People will be able to download the presentation and view it without Martin being present.*

Describe THREE ways that Martin could adapt his presentation so that it can be used when he is not present.

Presentation Software

Q1 Which of the following would be a suitable font size
for the bullet points in a presentation slide show?

    a)   3

    b)   30

    c)   300

Q2 Copy and complete the following sentence about
designing a presentation, using the words in the box.

You should decide on the format of the presentation; decide whether you'll be delivering it

.... or making it available as a ....

in person   computer file

Q3 Copy out the following sentences, picking out the correct word from each pair.

    a)   As a rough guide, there should be no more than **(six / sixty)** words
in a line of text on a slide.

    b)   As a rough guide, there should be no more than **(twenty / five)** lines of text on a slide.

    c)   As a rough guide, each slide should be visible for approximately **(two / five)** minutes
in a ten minute presentation.

    d)   It's a **(good / bad)** idea to use a different background and different font styles
on each slide in a presentation.

Q4 Write down TWO advantages and TWO disadvantages of using presentation software.

Q5 *Barry Trotter has produced a presentation about dinosaurs. Barry says "Everything I know
about dinosaurs has been put onto the slides. I won't need to tell the audience anything else."*

Write down ONE reason why Barry's decision may not be a good one.

Q6 *Paul Table has produced a presentation on the topic of 'Famous chairs in History'.
Paul has not put an opening or closing slide into his presentation.*

Give Paul one reason why he should use an opening slide
and one reason why he should use a closing slide.

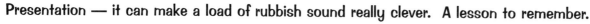

The key to ICT, revision and life in general...

Presentation — it can make a load of rubbish sound really clever. A lesson to remember.

Section Five — Spreadsheets and Databases

Spreadsheets — The Basics

Q1 Copy and complete the following sentences using these words.

> display   process   ordered   numbers
> graphs   text   calculations   search   charts

    a) A spreadsheet is a program that can ...... and ...... data in an ...... way.

    b) A spreadsheet can process both ...... and ....

    c) Spreadsheets can do ....

    d) Spreadsheets can ...... for particular items of data.

    e) Spreadsheets can produce ...... and ......

Q2 Copy the small spreadsheet. On your diagram draw labels to identify the rows, columns and cells. Write down the coordinates of the cell containing the question mark.

	A	B	C	D
1				
2			?	
3				

Q3 Study the following sentences and decide which are true. Copy the true statements.

    a) Each cell in a spreadsheet can contain text data, numerical data or formulas.

    b) If you type 732kg into a cell, that cell will have a numerical value of 732.

    c) Some spreadsheets recognize dates and money and convert them into a suitable format.

    d) It is not possible to sort text data into alphabetical order.

Q4 *Hard-Jet Airways use a spreadsheet to control the baggage check-in for each flight. Draw a section of a spreadsheet to show how the following data might appear:*

> **Passenger Name, Alcock, Brown, Wright, Baggage Number, 10796, 10797, 10798, Weight, 66kg, 25kg, 50kg.**

Q5   a) Three of the cells in the spreadsheet below contain incorrect mixed data. Write down the cell reference for each one.

    b) Explain why the date of birth column cells can display mixed data.

    c) Re-draw the spreadsheet correcting the errors.

	A	B	C	D
1	Name	Date Of Birth	Height	Weight
2				
3	David	23-Jun-75	1.6m	60
4	Ryan	16-Mar-80	1.7	55kg
5	Rio	11-Jul-77	1.8	70kg

Spreadsheets — Simple Formulas

Q1 Copy and complete the following sentences using the words below.

    a)   A formula is a ..... computer ....

    b)   A formula tells the computer to ..... data held in specific cells.

    c)   A formula uses .... which you can either type or select from a ..... .

functions   **process**   **program**   **list**   **simple**

Q2 Draw a simple table to show which of the following symbols are used for the listed functions.

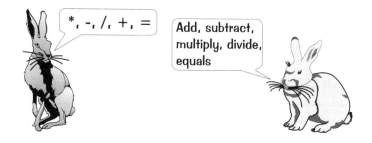

*, -, /, +, =

Add, subtract, multiply, divide, equals

Q3 For the data contained in the following spreadsheet, explain in simple steps what you would do to enter a formula in cell I2 to calculate the total weekly sales of the latest S Club album.

	A	B	C	D	E	F	G	H	I
1	**Album Artists**	**M**	**T**	**W**	**TH**	**F**	**S**	**SUN**	**TOTAL**
2	**S Club**	50	40	30	80	52	100	0	
3	**Ronan Keating**	10	10	12	13	14	25	0	
4	**Atomic Kitten**	20	23	22	21	24	30	0	
5	**Shaggy**	60	61	59	70	66	120	0	

Q4 In the above example you could copy the formula that you wrote to calculate S Club's sales and paste it into the total column for each of the other artists.

    a)   Would this give the correct solution?

    b)   Which type of cell reference would you be using, relative or absolute?

Q5 *The shopkeeper now wishes to calculate how much money he should have taken for each album. He changes the album price from time to time so decides to have a special cell to represent the price. (All the albums are priced the same.)*

    a)   Re-draw the spreadsheet to show how this would be included.

    b)   Write down the formula that would be used to calculate the value of sales of the Shaggy album.

    c)   Is the reference to your 'price' cell a relative or an absolute reference?

Spreadsheets — Charts and Graphs

Q1 Five of the following sentences link together to explain how to create a chart or graph from a spreadsheet. Decide which are the correct five and write them down in order.

A Select the type of chart you want.

B Multiply column A by column B.

C Decide whether the chart needs a key.

D Change all relative cell references to absolute.

E Get all the data you want to use in a single block.

F Highlight the data you want to use.

G Choose a good title for the chart and label any axes.

Q2 The table to the right is jumbled up. Re-draw the table so that it correctly shows the best uses of the charts and graphs, and examples of them.

Type	Best for	Example
Bar Graph	Continuous data on the x-axis	Shoe sizes of 50 people
Line Graph	Fractions of a total amount	Greenhouse temperature over the day
Scatter Graph	Separate data on the x-axis	Cola sales against hours of sunshine
Pie Chart	Showing relationships	Styles of music in the top forty

Q3 *Stefi is a tennis coach who has been offered sponsorship by five racket manufacturers. In order to help her to decide which to choose she has asked 60 tennis players which make they prefer. She has drawn up the spreadsheet shown below but wants to draw a chart or graph.*

a) Which type of graph or chart would you recommend?

b) Explain the steps Stefi would go through to produce the graph or chart using her spreadsheet program.

Make	Number of Users
Wilson	10
Head	20
Slazenger	15
Dunlop	5
Fischer	10
Total	**60**

Q4 *Samantha owns a small boutique. She is deciding what to buy for the coming season. She has data from last year on how many bikinis were sold in relation to the temperature of the day:*
$10°C — 1, 12°C — 2, 14°C — 3, 16°C — 5, 18°C — 10, 20°C — 30.$

a) Put the above data into a spreadsheet format.

b) Draw the graph which best represents this data.

Graphs Always Work Overtime...
If you need to see how something changes over time, always use a graph. If you need to see how something changes under time, look at the graph while hanging upside-down.

Spreadsheet Models and Simulations

Q1 Decide if each of these sentences is true or false. Copy out the true ones.

a) Spreadsheets can use formulas to describe the rules that real-world things seem to follow.

b) Spreadsheets can't be used to carry out what-if analysis.

c) Spreadsheets allow you to change input values to see the effect on the output.

d) The input values can be processed using formulas to produce output values.

Q2 Copy and complete the following sentences using the words from the box.

> input   output   modelling   charts   simulations   graphs

a) Spreadsheets can be used for ....

b) Spreadsheets can be used for ....

c) A spreadsheet model allows you to change the .... and see the effect on the ....

d) The output can be .... or .... which make predictions of the model easier to understand.

Q3 *Paula is a good 1500m runner. Her coach needs to advise her on tactics. She needs to be able to see the effect, on her total time, of running each of the four laps at a different pace.*

Draw a simple model that will allow her coach to carry out 'what-if' analysis of the effect that changing individual lap times will have on her total time.

Q4 *Ross is planning his autumn conker business. He has constructed a model that will allow him to see how it will affect his profits if he changes the number of conkers per bag, the price per bag or the number sold.*

	A	B
1	Number of bags sold	50
2	Number of conkers per bag	100
3	Price per bag p	100
4	Total money earned £	50
5	Money earned per conker p	1

Copy the model and write down the formulas that would appear in:

a) Cell B4

b) Cell B5

Q5 *'Italien Job Cars Ltd' specialise in servicing new Minis. Sergio must give a quality service with a quick turnaround. He constructs a model to show the relationship between the number of customers, number of mechanics, average time for 1 mechanic to service a mini and the total servicing time.*

> Hint: Assume that doubling the no. of mechanics halves the service time, etc.

Design a spreadsheet that he could use and write down the formula that relates to the cell containing '**total servicing time**'.

Databases

Q1 Look at the database shown below. Copy it out, and on your drawing:

Title	Author	ISBN	Date out	Due back
The Chamber of Secrets	Rowling	123456	10/11/2002	10/12/2002
The Lord of the Rings	Tolkien	321645	08/11/2002	08/12/2002
The Hobbit	Tolkien	654321	03/11/2002	03/12/2002
James and the Giant Peach	Dahl	152643	11/11/2002	11/12/2002

a) Identify the fields.

b) Identify the records.

c) Identify one item of data.

d) Identify the 'key field'.

Q2 Study the following sentences and copy out those that are true.

a) A database is an organised collection of data.

b) It is hard to find information in a large database.

c) Data is organised into fields and records.

d) It is quicker to keep manual records than to use a computer database.

e) A database can be used to generate reports.

Q3 Match each data type on the left with the correct data on the right.

Text   **1.3142**
Integer   **26/09/02**
Real Number   **Aardvark**
Date   **666**

Q4 Copy and complete the following sentences using the words on the field.

a) The first step in creating a database is to decide on what ...... you need.

b) Each field needs a ......, a description of its contents, a .... and a ....

c) The data type is important as different .... can be performed on different types of data.

d) The file size of the database can be reduced by .... data, eg. using 'M' and 'F' for male and female.

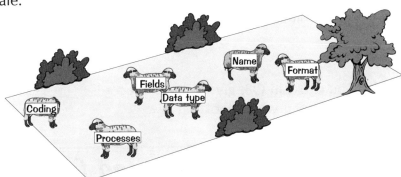

Q5 Write down the three important elements of a database.

Databases

Q6   *Mr Lloyd gives music lessons. He keeps information about his pupils on a database. The table below shows some of the fields that he uses. The grades are numbered 1-8 and the fee is in pounds.*

First Name	Last Name	Date of Birth	Grade	Instrument	Fee

Copy the table and below each field write down the data
type that he uses. ie Text, Real Number, Integer or Date.

Q7   *Riverdance is a dancing school specialising in folk dancing.*
A part of their database is shown below:

	A	B	C	D	E	F	G
1	First Name	Last Name	Gender	Type of Dance	Grade	Special Merit	Fee
2							
3	Claudia		Girl	Irish	Level 8	Distinction	25 Pounds
4							

Devise a system of coding for data in columns C to G that will reduce the file size and therefore
take up less computer memory. Copy out the database, writing your new coding into row 3.

Q8   *Caroline plays the flute. She keeps a record of the pieces that she has learnt and the date she learnt them. She plays jazz, classical and pop. She also records the name of the composer.*

Design a well-structured database for Caroline by:

a)   Deciding what fields she needs.

b)   Giving each field a name.

c)   Describing the contents of each field.

d)   Deciding what the format will be.

e)   Deciding what the data type is.

Q9   Using the fields that you chose in Q8, give 3 sample records
for the database to show how it would look.

Stuck in his tiny Cell, No.6 longed for open Fields...

They're interesting, charming, and can do your accounts for you. You won't have to buy them
chocolates, or remember their birthday. Go on, date a base.

Databases

Q10 *Farmer Mike is to start keeping information about his dairy herd on his farm computer. The table below shows one typical entry.*

Field name:								
Typical entry:	Mary	1056789	Friesian	21/03/2001	60 litres	998.5 kg	£120	£50
Data type:								
Coded:								

Copy out the table.

a)   Complete the top row of the table by suggesting field names for each piece of data.

b)   Complete the third row by writing down the data type for each field ie. text / integer / real number / date.

c)   Complete the bottom row by suggesting suitable coding for the data in each column. If coding is not suitable enter 'none'.

Q11 *A large department store uses a database to monitor its departmental sales performance. A typical week's report is shown below.*

	A	B	C	D
	Department	**This Week's Sales**	**Last Week's Sales**	**Difference**
1	Perfume	£10,000	£9,000	Up
2	Lingerie	£8,000	£7,000	Up
3	Toys	£6,000	£5,000	Up
4	Electrical	£20,000	£15,000	Up
5	Menswear	£12,000	£13,000	Down

a)   What is the key field?

b)   Could staff search the database to find the sales figures for their specific department?

c)   What would you do to sort the departments into alphabetical order?

d)   What would you do to sort the data so that the department with the highest takings this week is at the top of the database?

e)   Using the data above, give...

(At this point the writer of question 11 became de-motivated and refused to continue. Please proceed directly to Q12 on page 36. Do not pass Go. Do not collect £200.)

Databases

Q12 *The local leisure centre uses a computer to monitor the activities of its members. Mark, Gabby and Jacob are typical members. We know the following information about each of them: Gabby Smith has membership number 161. She swims, plays squash and uses the sauna. Jacob Jones has membership number 263. He plays badminton, swims and uses the gym. Mark Brown has membership number 111. He plays raquetball, swims and uses the gym.*

    a)   Draw a well-structured database to store this information.

    b)   What would be the key field?

Q13 Construct and draw out a database to record the fortunes of 5 hockey teams in a local league. It will have to record the number of matches played, number won, lost and drawn, points to date, goals for and goals against together with the current positions in the table.

Q14 *When prisoners arrive at Longstay Prison, their names are recorded and they are given a 5 digit prisoner number. The nature of their offence, their date of entry and length of sentence are also recorded.*

    a)   Construct and draw a memory efficient database to store the records and populate it with 3 imaginary prisoners' data.

    b)   What would be the key field?

    c)   What data type would the key field be?

And behold! The great beast was vanquished...

Rest easy friends, for the beast of databases has been impale-ed by the mighty CGP sword of knowledge. Rejoice ye one and all, and pour thy self a flagon.

Internet Basics

Q1 Copy and complete the following sentences using the words in the box below.

> | | |
> |---|---|
> | **Internet Service Provider** | **E-mail Client** |
> | **Web Browser**   **PC** | **Telephone Line** |

a) To connect to the Internet, you use your modem to dial up

a computer owned by an .... (ISP).

b) Most people use a .... (or Mac) and a normal .... to access the Internet.

c) The two most important pieces of software you need are a .... to display the web pages

and an .... which transmits and receives e-mail.

Q2 a) Copy and label the diagram using the words in the box below.

b) Explain what a modem does.

c) What is an ISP?

d) What two pieces of software would be required in order to access the WWW and to be able to send and receive emails?

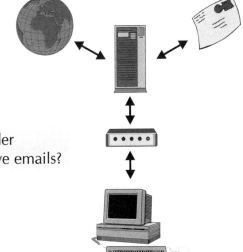

> | | | |
> |---|---|---|
> | **Modem** | **ISP** | **E-mail** |
> | **World Wide Web** | **Computer** | |

Q3 Complete sentences a), b) and c) using the phrases in the box to the right.

a) **Internet research is a** ....

b) **Making a web page is a** ....

c) **Using e-mail is a** ....

> **quick way to send messages.**
>
> **good way to find information from around the world.**
>
> **great way to tell the world who you are and what you think.**

Q4 *Colin is moving house. He would like to keep in touch with his friends, but has a phobia of telephones. He decides to keep in touch with them using the Internet.*

What hardware and software should Colin get?

Researching a Topic

Q1   Give **one** advantage and **one** disadvantage of using each of the sources below for research.

a)   **Books**   b)   **CD-ROMs**   c)   **The Internet**

Q2   Say if each of the following sentences is true or false.

a)   You can search for information on the Internet with a scratch enzyme.

b)   Search Engines are websites that help you to search for other websites.

c)   Oggle, Yah Boo, Labrador, Depress and Tell Nell are all popular search engines.

d)   When you type a keyword into a search engine, it lists a load of websites containing that word.

e)   Complex searches can be carried out by using more than one keyword and linking them together with AND and OR.

Q3   Copy out the paragraph below about search engines, picking out the correct word from each pair in brackets.

Search engines store (**locks** / **keywords**) of different websites. When you search, you get a list of possible (**web pages** / **keys**) with your (**lock** / **keyword**) in. These are called (**hits** / **cookies**). The search engine will often find thousands of (**hits** / **cookies**), but it only displays about (**10** / **200**) at a time. Different search engines tend to produce (**the same** / **different**) results, so if you can't find what you want, it's worth trying a few different ones.

Q4   *Sarah is part of the Craig David Appreciation Society. She has entered David as a keyword in one of her search engines and a list of hits has been displayed.*

a)   Other than the ranking, name 3 things that the list might tell her about each page.

b)   The list displays the following in blue underlined text:
http://www.flava.co.uk?
What three letters are used to describe this?

Tell me what's your search engine...Oooo

You've gotta search for the keyword inside yourself...

Search engines usually have a "help page" or a page with tips on searching. They'll tell you how to do more complicated searches, like searching for things only in certain languages.

Searching for Information

Q1 Copy and complete the following sentences using the words in the box:

a) A list of hits might contain .... of websites.

b) You need to pick out the ones that are likely to be ....

c) Look at the details ....

d) Looking at the page's URL can give you a good idea of its ....

e) The .... can give you some idea who wrote the site.

content
useful
millions
URL
in order

Q2 Using the words below, copy and complete the following sentences about how to navigate the web.

a) Browsers can save URLs that you use often in a feature called .... or ....

b) .... are often coloured blue and underlined.

c) Browsers keep a list of all the websites you've visited — this is called the ....

d) Browsers have .... and .... buttons. These let you retrace your steps to go back to a page you saw earlier and then go forwards again.

Q3 Say which of the following sentences are true and which are false.

a) Hyperlinks are the bits on a web page that you can click on to go somewhere else.

b) The pointer changes to a foot when you hover over a hyperlink.

c) Hyperlinks are often displayed in a different colour if you've used them before.

d) Pressing the history button will take you to a GCSE History website.

Q4 *Some time ago, Jenny's best friend gave her the details of a specialist website about spinning. Jenny visited the site on her own computer and then threw away the paper containing its details.*

a) How could she get back to the website without asking her friend?

b) Once back on the website, what could she do to ensure that she could find it again easily?

Browsers — what a lot to learn...

I thought of a URL joke — something about URL-ton John, you know, like Elton John. But it was bad. It was terrible. Oh dear. Oh dear... Oh dear. Oh dear. Oh dear. Oh dear. Oh dear.

Searching for Information

Q1 Ollie wants to start his first chicken hotel, but doesn't have any chickens.
He has located a website that might be of some help.

Which of these things could help him find the information he wants within the website?

    a)   The website's list of contents

    b)   The favourites folder

    c)   Ollie's pet French cabbage, Amelie

    d)   The site map

    e)   The history window

Q2 The following jumbled sentences describe how you would keep information
that you find on the Internet. Unscramble each one and write it down correctly.

    a)   text bit of interesting When you find an, or a picture good, save it you'll probably want to.

    b)   file menu Use the page whole to the save.

    c)   Instead saving of the whole page, or all it out printing,
you can save just the you need bits.

    d)   picture good you find a If, click it on right, and paste and copy it into program graphics a.

Q3 Say if each of these is true or false.

    a)   When you save something from the Internet, it's a good idea
to make a note of the URL where you found it.

    b)   There is no need to tell people where you got your information.

    c)   An easy way to keep a note of things that you find is to
copy the website address from the Address Bar.

    d)   You get lots of respect from your mates by pretending that ideas you got from the web
were actually your own and you may eventually be made Prime Minister.

Q4 Anne has been doing research for an English project. She has discovered a 'Lakeland Poets'
website that has some good text and a nice picture of a really hairy poet that she wants to keep.

    a)   Explain how she could save the text she wants for later use.

    b)   Explain how she could save the picture for later use.

    c)   What should she do in order to keep a log of what she found?

Fact and Opinion

Q1   Use these words to copy and complete the following sentences:

biased	fair	facts	ignored	anyone

a)   Information you find on the Internet could be ....

b)   Biased information supports a particular view without being ....

c)   Some facts might be .... because they don't fit in with the writer's opinion.

d)   People often claim biased opinions are ...., even when they aren't facts at all.

e)   Because .... can put information on the Internet, a lot of it is untrue.

Q2   Say which of the following are true and which are false.

a)   People might write a biased article because they want to support a political party.

b)   Most people are never biased.

c)   People might use the Internet to convince other people to believe the same as they do.

Q3   Say which of the following are **Primary Data** and which are **Secondary Data.**

a)   Enrique Inglesias — the world's greatest solo artist.

b)   This month's rainfall.

c)   Number of births in the UK this week.

d)   Mobile phones flatten your ears.

Q4   *Danny found the following skateboarding sites on the Internet.*
boardnews.co.uk — Articles about boards.
whichskateboard.co.uk — Comparison of all boards available in UK.
ourboardsarebest.com — American manufacturer's site.
USAboarddata.org — Compiled by research students at UCLA.
fastestlightest.co.uk — Dimensions, weights, & other performance figures listed.

a)   Which site would you expect to be the most biased?

b)   Which site(s) would you expect to contain Primary data?

c)   Which site(s) would you expect to contain Secondary data?

d)   Which site(s) would you expect to contain statistics?

Fun? ... Bias it is.

It's not that bad this lot. Bias, fact, opinion ... it's basically common sense. Just remember to be a bit suspicious of stuff you come across on the Internet, and of men with ear hair, of course.

Design a Web Page

Q1   Copy and complete the following sentences using the words below.

interesting		fonts		long
minimum		hyperlinks	simple	pictures

a)   Websites need to be .... to read.

b)   Web pages should be clear and use a small number of ....

c)   Ensure that you keep your design ....

d)   .... make a web page interesting, but take a .... time to download.

e)   .... should be kept to a ....

Q2   The web page shown to the right is poorly designed.
Say how you would do each of the following things:

a)   Improve the appearance of the title.

b)   Reduce the download time.

c)   Make the site clearer.

d)   Make it easy for people to move to other pages.

Dead duck Internet design

We specialise in dead boring websites.

Our sites are renowned for their lack of impact and thoroughly boring content they contain very very long sentences that mean very little and indeed can confuse many people.

Q3   Say whether each of these sentences is true or false.

a)   Web pages are just like books, you start at page one and read all the pages in order.

b)   Web pages have buttons so that you can choose what you want to read.

c)   Most people are interested in the same things.

d)   You can have lots of buttons or hyperlinks on your web page,
all linking to different pages.

Q4   *Victoria's hobby is keeping small, furry animals. She is proud of her collection
and is designing a website to tell fellow enthusiasts about it.*

She requires help with designing her first page. Draw out the page
to show her how each of the following should appear:

a)   Title: **Small and Furry Animals.**

b)   Sub title: **Vicky's collection.**

c)   Her two pictures — one of a hamster, one of a rabbit.

d)   Background colour and text colour.

Hamster & Rabbit

Small and Furry Animals

Vicky's Collection

Creating a Web Page

Q1   Look at the tool bar below. Say which button you would press to do each of the following:

a)   set the type of font

b)   underline the highlighted text

c)   format a whole paragraph

d)   change the size of highlighted text

Q2   Copy and complete the following sentences using the words in the box:

Insert	numbered	background	bulleted

a)   A list that looks like

> •   bla bla blaaaab
> •   bllllaaa bliaaaa

is called a .... list.

b)   A list that looks like

> 1)   blabaty bla bla
> 2)   bla blab blabay

is called a .... list.

c)   Changing the .... of a web page is easy — just choose a colour or picture.

d)   By using the .... menu, you can easily add horizontal lines.

Q3   a)   How would you add a picture to your web page?

b)   What would you use to get your pictures to appear in the right place on your web page?

c)   What are the two main types of picture used on the Internet? Pick them out from the list below.

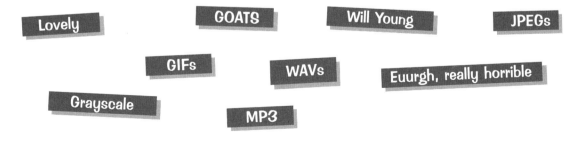

Creating a Web Page — the Harder Bits

Q1 Put the 3 sentences below into the right order, so that
they correctly describe how to make a link for a web page.

A   Select the button and make it a link by clicking on the hyperlink button.

B   Type the address of the page that you want to link to in the box marked 'URL'.

C   Create the word, shape or picture that you want to use as the button.

Q2 Copy and complete the following sentences, choosing
the correct word from the three choices for each:

a)   .... is the language of the WWW.   **(C++)**   **(HTML)**   **(BASIC)**

b)   .... software allows you to produce web pages without knowing HTML.
       (spreadsheet)   **(badger)**   **(web-design)**

c)   To see what HTML looks like, click on the view menu and choose ....
       (source)   **(ketchup)**   **(spring)**

Q3 Three column headings are shown in bold below. Draw a table using these headings and
insert the words from the box into the correct columns to show the relationship between them.

IMAGE QUALITY   FILE SIZE   DOWNLOAD TIME

good	poor	slow
quick	small	large

Q4 Say whether each of the following is refering to a GIF or a JPEG.

a)   ..... files are better for photographs.
b)   ..... files are best for simple pictures with few colours eg logos and line drawings.
c)   ..... files can display more colours.
d)   ..... files are often used for simple animations.
e)   ..... rhymes with "whiff".

Q5 *Miss Bounce is planning an aerobics class. She is putting her
lessons on the school website so that her students can try the
moves at home. She draws five pictures of the basic positions:*

a)   What should she save them as?

b)   What does she need to do now to
       make them into an animated GIF?

Variety — the spice of life...

Try revising in lycra — it really breaks up the day. Look how happy these lot are.
But then they could be happy for a number of reasons. They could be insane.

Design a Website

Q1   The spider chart below is going to show the types of pages in a website.
     Copy it out and label it to show what is in each section using the words in the box.

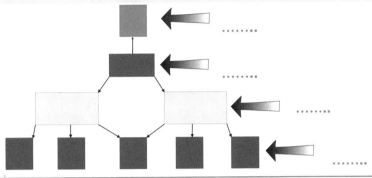

| Homepage | Links To Other Sites | Basic Information | More Advanced Information |

Q2   Say which of the following statements are true and which are false.

   a)   Libelling means to publish something untrue about a person.

   b)   There is nothing to prevent you from saying untrue things
        about a person that damages their reputation.

   c)   Libelling means printing addresses onto small sticky backed
        pieces of paper that can be affixed to envelopes.

   d)   There are libel laws to prevent you publishing things that are untrue about people.

   e)   People who break libel laws can be taken to court and forced to pay large fines.

Q3   Draw a table with two columns called **Dos** and **Don'ts.**
     Place items from the list below into the correct column.

     Copy somebody else's work without acknowledging it.
     Use somebody else's words but write down who said it.
     Acknowledge somebody's copyright.
     Avoid plagiarism.
     Tell lies about people.

Q4   *Nicholas and David have been asked to design a website for their town orchestra.*

     Draw a spider chart to show how the following information might be organised:

     Mint town Youth Orchestra
     String, brass, percussion sections
     Names of players in each section
     Pictures of the instruments in each section

I hate spiders charts — they're so creepy and... eurrgh...
It's pretty important to acknowledge whee you get all your information from.
You wouldn't want to be sued. Did I say "whee"? Oops. I meant widget. (I think.)

E-Mail

Q1 Copy the diagram below and write in the 5 steps for sending an email message.

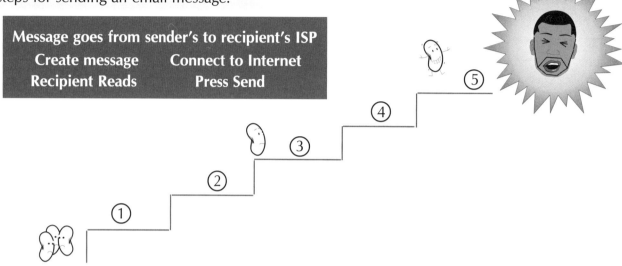

> Message goes from sender's to recipient's ISP
> Create message   Connect to Internet
> Recipient Reads   Press Send

Q2 a) What is web based e-mail?

b) Name **one** major web based e-mail provider.

Q3 Copy and complete these sentences using the words from the box below.

a) It's possible to send .... via e-mail.

b) Files sent by e-mail are called ....

c) Unless you are expecting an attachment, treat any that you receive with ....

d) It's easy to get a .... from an infected attachment.

e) You can use virus checking software to .... an attachment before downloading it.

files	scan	attachments	virus	suspicion

Q4 *Mr Woolly has run his tea-cosy business without the aid of a computer for over sixty years. He has employed a new manager, Bob, who is keen to use e-mail.*

Listed below are some of the arguments used against e-mail by Mr Woolly. Write down a counter argument that Bob could use for each statement:

a) It is difficult to send e-mail.

b) I can only send messages.

c) E-mails that I receive will have viruses.

d) The equipment and software that I need is expensive to buy.

e) It will take forever to send our newsletter via e-mail.

Address Books

Q1 What is an e-mail address book?

Q2 *James has sent me an e-mail from his work address jamesisworking@loa.com.*

Which of the following would be the quickest way to add his address to my address book?

a) Type it in very carefully.

b) Copy it and paste it into my address book.

c) Right click on the message and choose 'add sender to address book'.

Q3 *Sula keeps the e-mail addresses of all her friends and acquaintances in her address book. She likes knitting, heavy metal and Gareth Gates. She wants to have her friends round in the holidays but knows that the three groups of friends don't mix.*

a) What could she set up to ensure that e-mail invitations only went to members of one group of friends?

b) How would she be able to write one invitation but send it to all the members of a group?

c) She has some friends who do share more than one interest. Could they be included in each group?

Q4 Say which of the following statements are true and which are false.

a) E-mail address books can contain e-mail addresses, but no other information.

b) To add the e-mail address of someone who has just sent me an e-mail, I can right click and choose 'Add sender to address book'.

c) I can only send e-mail to one person at a time.

d) When you send an e-mail to a group it goes to all the people in the group.

Q5 *Amy wants to swap gossip over the Internet about Soaps. She has some friends who like Stolen Moments and some who like Peachy Street. She sets up two e-mail groups called Stolen Moments and Peachy Street.*

a) What will the group called 'Stolen Moments' have in it?

b) What will happen when she sends an e-mail to 'Peachy Street'?

c) What's the next section in this book called? Pick the correct answer from those below. (No peeking.)

Section 7 — Kylie and Britney

Section 7 — More databases cos you love em

Section 7 — Computers in the Real World

Section 7 — I want my mummy

Computers in Shops

Q1 What do each of the following stand for?

a) EPOS   b) EFTPOS

Q2 Use the words below to copy and complete the following sentences:

products	laser scanner	contains details	Bar codes

a) .... look like this. ▷ ▌▌▌ ▌▌▌

b) A bar code .... about the product.

c) Bar codes can be found on most ....

d) A .... on the till scans the bar code details into the system.

Q3 Say whether the following sentences about a supermarket are likely to be true or false.

a) The laser scanner is connected to the store's computer which contains the prices of all the products.

b) The stock controller, Sally, counts the stock after each sale.

c) The price that relates to the bar code of a scanned item is passed back to the till by the computer.

d) The assistant writes the prices down and gives them to the customer as a receipt.

e) The till processes and prints the customer's receipt.

Q4 *Pets 'R' Us is a large retail pet supermarket that uses an EPOS system. Every product is bar coded and all the prices are held on a central computer. The number of units of each product in the shop and warehouse is also centrally stored.*

a) What is the name for the goods in the warehouse and shop? (Clue: It rhymes with frock.)

b) If somebody buys a Rock Chew, what will the computer do besides reading the bar code and passing the price to the till?

c) What will happen when the number of Rock Chews in the warehouse falls below the re-order level?

Q5 *'We are Huge' Supermarkets Ltd has an EFTPOS system.*

a) What does EFTPOS allow customers to do instead of paying in cash?

b) How are details of the card holder stored on the card?

c) How is this information taken off the card?

d) A payment request is made via a telephone network. What happens if the card is valid?

e) Why do debit and credit cards have a space for the customer's signature?

More Computer Applications

Q1 Copy and complete the following sentences about weather forecasting using Dick's face tattoos.

a) .... is usually collected by sensors from an automated .... system.

b) Data is processed to produce a .... of the area using a geographical information system.

c) A series of images collected at different times can be used to create a kind of .... of the weather systems.

d) The data can also be fed into a .... of the way weather patterns change — to make a more detailed forecast.

Q2 Study the following sentences about traffic management in a car park. Say which are true and which are false.

a) Staff at the entrance and exits of a car park count the cars as they go in and out, work out if there are spaces and key the information into a electronic sign.

b) Some busy towns have car park management systems.

c) Sensors at the entrances and exits of many car parks are used to calculate how many spaces are left in each car park.

d) Information from sensors is stored in the car park computer and electronic parking signs on nearby roads are updated every hour.

e) Motorists see the signs, that are updated in real time, and don't have to waste time driving to a car park that is already full.

Q3 *Sports Direct wants to encourage customers to return to their stores. They want to know what each customer buys, how much they spend and when they shop. They will then reward their good customers with gifts, special offers or vouchers.*

a) What sort of scheme would they need to set up on the shop's computer?

b) What would each customer be given?

c) Typically, what information would be kept on a customer's loyalty card?

d) What happens when a customer's loyalty card is swiped at the checkout?

e) How does this information help the shop to control stock?

Free toad polisher when you spend £500 on hair wax...

So, a loyalty scheme means you get money off and stuff. Great. But on the other hand, the shops know who you are and what you bought. A bit weird. If you were paranoid, you'd feel spied-on.

Even More Computer Applications

Q1   Write down the two types of electronic kiosk.

Q2   Draw a table with column headings **POINT OF SALE** and **POINT OF INFORMATION**.
      Copy the phrases below (on the frog's tongue) under the correct heading.

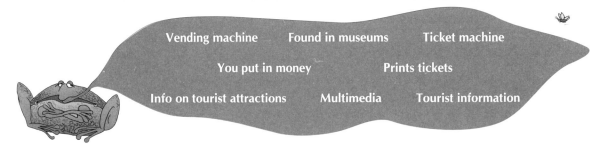

Vending machine   Found in museums   Ticket machine
You put in money   Prints tickets
Info on tourist attractions   Multimedia   Tourist information

Q3   a)   What is the diagram shown below called?

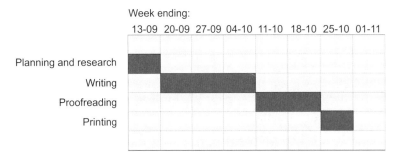

Week ending:
13-09 20-09 27-09 04-10 11-10 18-10 25-10 01-11

Planning and research
Writing
Proofreading
Printing

      b)   Copy out the following sentences, unjumbling the underlined words.

      i)   The diagram above is a kind of <u>dusclhee</u> for working out how long a project will take.

      ii)   The project is broken down into <u>cicifspe</u> <u>staks</u>.

      iii) You input <u>owh</u> <u>nglo</u> each task will take.

Q4   *Dull City's museum has thousands of black and white photographs*
      and drawings that it doesn't have enough room to display.

      a)   What computer driven application could they install to overcome the problem?

      b)   What specific type of screen would make the device more attractive?

      c)   Name two things that the device could run that would make the display more fun for kids.

Q5   *Think of six tasks that you do each morning between*
      waking up and leaving the house for school or college.

      a)   Write down each of the tasks and how long you think it will take to complete.

      b)   Draw out a schedule with the six tasks down the side and the time of day across the top.

      c)   What is this type of diagram called?

      d)   Draw in the bars for each of your tasks.

Measurement — Data Logging

Q1 Choose the correct words from the pairs to complete these sentences about using sensors.

a) (**Infra-red** / **Sound**) sensors can be used to check that aircraft noise is within agreed levels.
b) (**Air pressure** / **Light**) sensors are used to control emergency oxygen masks on aircrafts.
c) (**Light-dependent resistors** / **Thermistors**) control when to switch street lights on.
d) (**Pressure sensors** / **Thermistors**) are used to control air-conditioning systems.
e) An infra-red sensor can detect a break in an infra-red beam
— this is used in (**human brains** / **burglar alarms**).
f) (**Infra-red sensors** / **Geiger counters**) measure the amount of radioactivity in an object.

Q2 Say which of the following sentences are true and which are false.

a) Data logging means capturing all data from a timber factory.
b) Data logging is best when only small amounts of data need to be collected.
c) Data logging is the process of collecting and storing data and then downloading it into a computer program for analysis.
d) Data logging is not necessary when data needs collecting from hostile environments.
e) Data logging means capturing and storing information using sensors.

Q3 Copy and complete the following sentences using these words.

> input sensor   Digital   Analogue
> analogue-to-digital converter   CSV

a) Data is collected by an ....
b) .... sensors can usually only be **ON** or **OFF**.
c) .... sensors can take a range of values.
d) Before an analogue signal can be downloaded and stored on a computer system, it needs to be converted to a digital signal using an ....
e) Digital data can be stored in .... format so that it can be exported into a spreadsheet for analysis.

Q4 *Kumala is in charge of her school's weather station. So that she doesn't have to go out in bad weather to read the wind speed gauge, she is setting up a data logging system linked to a computer.*

a) Would she use an analogue or a digital sensor?
b) Explain your answer to part a).
c) What would she need in order to download the data onto the computer system?
d) What type of format would the data be saved in so that it could be exported to a spreadsheet for analysis?

Logging Period and Logging Interval

Q1 Copy out these sentences, replacing the logs and small creatures with words from the box.

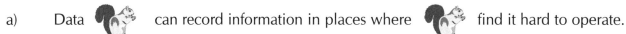

| short logging long humans sleep rapidly Intervals changing |

a)   Data [squirrel] can record information in places where [squirrel] find it hard to operate.

b)   Data can be collected over very [skull] or very [skull] periods — you could record the growth rate of a tree or the [skull] [skull] temperature inside a nuclear explosion.

c)   [log] between the measurements are more precise than when a human's doing the measuring.

d)   Data loggers don't need tea breaks, lunch breaks or [log] .

Q2 Draw a table with column headings **LONG INTERVAL** and **SHORT INTERVAL**. Enter the phrases below under the correct heading.

growth of a whale   **temperature of an explosion**
height of a sunflower   **lean of the famous Leaning Tower of Millom**
speed of a bullet   **temperature of a cake during cooking**

Q3 Say which of the following statements are true and which are false.

a)   The logging period is the total length of time you're going to collect data.

b)   The logging period is always one minute.

c)   If you're not sure what logging period to use, do some preliminary research.

d)   It doesn't matter if the period is too short or too long, the computer will adjust the figures.

e)   If the period is too long, you can waste valuable time.

f)   If the period is too short, you can miss important data.

Q4 *Una Hake keeps tropical fish in a tank at home. She is going to transfer the fish for 3 hours to a temporary tank whilst she repairs the main one. The fish can only live in a water temperature between 10 and 30 degrees centigrade. If the temperature goes outside of either of these limits for more than one minute the fish could die. She attaches a sensor to the tank in order to measure the water temperature.*

a)   Write down a formula that shows the relationship between **logging period**, **logging interval** and **number of readings**.

b)   Choose a suitable logging period.

c)   Choose a suitable logging interval.

d)   Calculate how many readings she will take.

Measuring Physical Data

Q1   Below are six questions you should ask yourself when using ICT to measure physical data.
     Copy and complete each sentence using the words in the thought cloud.

   a)   How long are you going to .... for?

   b)   What .... do you want the data in?

   c)   Is there more than one .... occurring?

   d)   How .... do the measurements have to be taken?

   e)   Is it a .... of events?

   f)   Is it a .... event?

measure   often
change   sequence
unique   format

Q2   *A geologist is planning to measure the temperature of lava during a volcanic eruption.*

     Below are a number of factors that he should consider before starting.
     Write down what you would answer to each one.

   a)   Is there more than thing to measure?

   b)   Is it a sequence of events, or are you measuring one thing continuously?

   c)   Is it a unique event?

   d)   For how long will the measurements take place — a day, a month or a year?

   e)   How often do the measurements need to be taken
        — every minute, every hour or every day?

   f)   What format should the data be in?

Q3   *A.V. Ation Ltd is doing an investigation into noise levels from aircraft.*
     They are monitoring noise and height and speed of the aircraft for a month.

     Their research engineer considers the following questions.
     Write down what you would answer to each one.

   a)   Is there more than one thing to measure?

   b)   Is it a sequence of events or are you measuring one thing continuously?

   c)   Is it a unique event?

   d)   For how long will the measurements take place?

   e)   How often do the measurements need to be taken?

   f)   What format should the data be in?

Ask yourself six questions...

How? Why? When? Where? What? Who? When measuring physical data, be clear on what
you need to know.

Answers: lead piping for the money, last night, in the drawing room, murder, Miss Scarlet.

Computers and the Law

Q1   Copy and complete the following sentences using Bob's words.

eight, fine, anyone, compensation, personal, principles

(Bob doesn't like words.)

a)   The Data Protection Act gives rights to .... who has data about them stored on a computer.

b)   The law allows people to see the .... data stored about them.

c)   The act consists of .... data protection ....

d)   Breaking this law can lead to a .... and being made to pay ....

Q2   Use Bob's words to make sentences describing four ways that the Copyright Act can be broken.

a)   Using .... without a proper ....

b)   Downloading text or images from the internet and using them without saying where you got them, or without receiving the copyright owner's ....

copies, licence, copyright, permission, software, copying,

c)   .... a computer program you use at work and running it on a computer at home without permission from the .... holder.

d)   Making .... of software and giving it to your friends.

Q3   Copy and complete the following sentences using the words attacking Bob, so that they describe activities which are illegal under the Computer Misuse Act:

a)   .... access to computer .... (eg. hacking).

b)   Gaining unauthorised access to a computer to carry out serious crimes like .... and ....

c)   Unauthorised changing of computer files including planting .... and deleting files.

Unauthorised, fraud, blackmail, viruses, files.

(Words don't like Bob)

Computers and the Workplace

Q1 Divide the jobs into those that have been replaced by computers and those that have been created by computers.

> Typists   Car assembly workers   Computer hardware designers
> Programmers   Systems analysts   Filing clerks   IT technicians

Q2 Say which of the following statements are true and which are false.

a) Hot-desking is when an employee sits at the desk nearest to the radiator.

b) Less office space is needed if employees hot-desk.

c) Teleworkers spend less time commuting.

d) Teleworking is another name for jobs in the manufacture of TV sets.

e) Teleworking can be lonely.

Q3 *In Sure Us is a growing insurance broker. Desmond has to persuade the partners that it would be good to install a computerised system. Using the words below, make up sentences to:*

a) explain how computers can change the amount of work done.

b) explain two types of work that the computer can do.

c) describe the jobs that are left for the employees to do.

d) describe the overall effect of computerisation on the business.

Increase, productive, competitive, boring, repetitive, interesting

Q4 *Following Desmond's presentation, the oldest and most senior partner of In Sure Us fights against his proposals. Using words from the list below, make up sentences to:*

a) Explain how computers can cause people to lose their jobs.

b) Explain how computers can be bad for employees.

c) Describe two difficulties with keeping up with the latest technology.

d) Describe what you need to do for your staff before they can use the computers.

replace, people, perform, very fast, health, problems, expensive, training, time, money.

Computer Use — Health and Safety Issues

Q1   Draw a table using the three complaints on the left as headings. Copy the solutions on the right into the correct columns. (Each solution can be used more than once).

Repetitive Strain Injury

Take regular breaks.
Proper chair and backrest.
Well-positioned keyboard.
Eye Strain and Headaches

Good background lighting.
A screen filter.
Wrist rests.
Circulation, Fitness and Back Problems.

Look away from the screen.
Walk around.

Q2   Choose from the list below three suitable phrases that describe the main problems connected with computer use and write them into a sentence that explains the problem.

> **Arthritis, Repetitive Strain Injury, insomnia, eye strain and headache, fitness, back pain and circulation, stroke, gout, warts, chipped nails, cheesy feet.**

Q3   Copy and complete the sentences below using the words from Ken's fat belly:

a)   Check that computer equipment and the work area is ....

b)   Ensure that workstations meet .... requirements.

c)   Employees must have regular ....

d)   Provide .... eye-tests for all staff who regularly use VDUs in their job.

e)   Provide health and safety .... and information so people can reduce the risks.

Q4   You have been asked to show stupid Dennis how to sit properly at the computer.
Write down advice to give him to help him protect the following parts of his body:

a)   Back
b)   Eyes
c)   Forearms
d)   Feet

Dennis

Q5   Dennis is stupid. He didn't listen to any advice, and is now complaining of the following problems.
For each complaint suggest a possible solution:

a)   My back hurts.

b)   I get terrible headaches.

c)   I get pins and needles in my legs.

d)   My wrists are very stiff.

e)   My nose has turned to clay.   *(I told you he was stupid)*

Microsoft Access Guide to Success

Learn in a Guided Way to Combine Inforr
Your Database, Optimize Your Task and P
Your Colleagues and Clients | Big Four Consulting Firms
Method

Copyright © 2022
Kevin Pitch

TABLE OF CONTENTS

INTRODUCTION...3

1   SOFTWARE INTERFACE AND USE..8

2   LET'S START...12

3   LET'S EXPLORE THIS IN DETAIL...22

4   REPORTS..28

5   QUESTIONS AND ANSWERS...32

6   THE BEST ACCESS PLUGINS..38

7   TIPS, TRICKS & FAQ WITH COMMON PROBLEMS AND SOLUTIONS....39

8   THE STRATEGIC SHORTCUTS...43

9   CONCLUSION..45

INTRODUCTION

While alternative databases are expensive, Microsoft Access is comparatively cheap. Additionally, it is a component of the Microsoft 365 software package. You may already own Microsoft Access, but if not, you can purchase it separately. The software is available in various editions, including standalone and free versions. You can also use Microsoft Access with other Microsoft programs, like Excel and Word.

There are many ways to use Microsoft Access to develop database applications. You don't need to be an expert to utilise it, and no programming skills are required. Instead, find out what it is, how to use it, and where you can purchase or download it. This book will cover the most critical aspects of using database software.

Microsoft Access is a business, personal, and academic database management system. It is the most widely used database in the world. Microsoft Access has a lot of features that make it easy to use. The software also has a lot of templates that can be customized to suit your needs.

We term MS Access as a relational database management system (RDBMS) initially designed for Windows. It offers a wide range of features, including data security and ease of use. As a database software, Microsoft Access helps users to manage and store information in a structured way. Many companies and organizations, including the US government, have used it. You can use Microsoft Access for personal and business purposes. It helps you to combine the information to create your database.

Microsoft Access is one of the world's most widely used software and has become an essential tool for many users. Individuals use Microsoft Access, small businesses, large corporations, and governments to manage their information.

Microsoft Access is a simple yet powerful tool that combines the information to create your database. Microsoft Access can help you create your database quickly and efficiently without much hassle. The software has a guided way of teaching new users how to use it and an algorithm that will help you optimize your task and project. It also guides how to combine information to create your database and optimize your tasks and project.

Access can be used in many ways, such as creating a database, importing data, or exporting it to other programs. It also offers a wide range of features that make it easy to do tasks like finding duplicates or calculating averages.

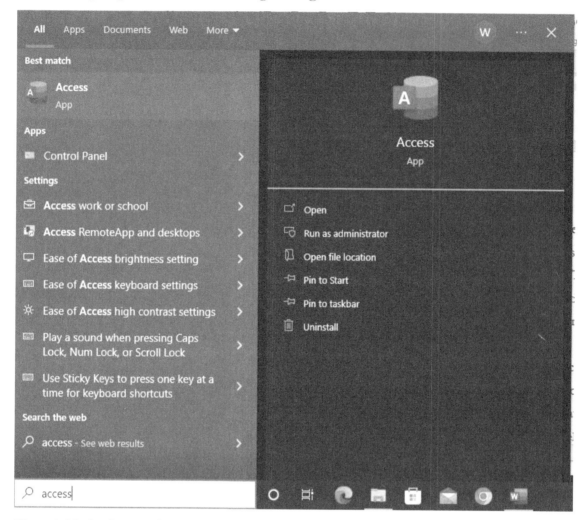

Figure 1: Navigating to MS Access

What is database & database development?

Microsoft Access provides a powerful tool for creating database objects. It offers various templates you can use as a starting point for your project. These templates are pre-built with the tables, forms, queries, and macros you need to create a custom database. You can use these templates to manage contacts, issues, or other information. Some of these templates even have sample records to help you get started.

The main purpose of a database is to organize data. Many people create databases in Access or Excel for personal use. These applications typically have short life cycles and are meant to be easy to manage for their creator. As such, most personal databases are not developed with advanced database concepts and are built by non-programmers. These databases are low-end, easy to maintain, and an excellent option for rapid application development.

While Access does not provide the utmost flexibility, it does provide many valuable tools to solve common database problems. It is also cheaper than more complex solutions and offers increased performance. The cost of a database solution can be a significant factor for an organization. However, it is essential to remember that different problems require different solutions.

Organizations change their database needs over time. The Microsoft Access platform is the most popular database application, and it can solve many problems for large and small organizations. But it is not a good database solution for every situation. Ultimately, Microsoft Access should be a part of an organization's overall database strategy.

Where can I buy or download Microsoft Access

Microsoft Access is a good choice if you're a business owner who needs to build database-heavy applications. It offers several tools and templates that let you build and edit apps easily. Access also allows you to automate various processes. It also integrates with Microsoft Azure, SQL Server, and Visual Basic. It's a powerful program that will enable you to create scalable and secure database management applications. It is beneficial for small and medium-sized businesses.

However, the program isn't free. You'll need to purchase Microsoft Access for your PC to use it. In addition, there is a challenge using the web app for this program, so you'll need a desktop computer to use it. You can also sign up for a Microsoft 365 subscription, allowing you to use Access for free for a certain period.

You may consider downloading the trial version if you're not a business owner but still want to use Microsoft Access. The software comes with many templates and comes with premium support. In addition, you can also access video tutorials and informative guides. Additionally, there's a frequently asked questions section that you can refer to for answers to common questions.

Microsoft's Office productivity suite has evolved over the years, and Microsoft Access is no exception. Microsoft Access was released back in 1992 and is among the most popular desktop database management systems (DBMS). It took Microsoft several years to develop and market a desktop database management system, but purchasing FoxPro helped accelerate the development process. In addition, by continuing to market FoxPro, Microsoft could use the database engine's source code and streamline the development process.

Where you can use Microsoft Access

Microsoft Access can be invaluable if you've been tasked with creating and maintaining business databases. This database software makes creating and maintaining a database a breeze, thanks to its easy-to-use interface. Users can import and export data easily with the help of the wizard built into the program. The wizard will also save the operation's details in a specification. Microsoft Access also includes templates to help users create and manage their databases.

Microsoft Access is available for download from Microsoft's website. Once you've downloaded the software, follow the installation steps. This database program is extremely powerful, making it ideal for organizing large amounts of data and creating custom forms and reports. Microsoft Office 365 subscribers can also use the Microsoft Access web app, which lets you work with your databases on any computer.

Microsoft Access is also helpful in schools, where it can simplify student information management. For example, it can send students emails, manage schedule changes and cancellations, and more. It can also be used to schedule and contact substitute teachers, which can help schools run more smoothly. The options are practically endless with Microsoft Access. This tool can help you organize your daily activities with ease. In addition, it is a powerful database management system that will help you run your business efficiently.

Microsoft Access allows you to integrate data from several sources, including Microsoft Office applications, SQL Servers, and Azure servers. It also offers many integration options with many other programs. If you are looking for an affordable database program, Access is a great option.

1 SOFTWARE INTERFACE AND USE

Ribbon

The ribbon contains a progression of order tabs containing the order. In Microsoft Access, the essential order tabs are Record, Home, Create, External Data, and Database tools. Each of the tabs contains a social event of related orders, and these get-togethers surface a piece of extra UI parts. The Tabs in Ribbon likewise mirror the right now dynamic article or data.

The Microsoft Access ribbon is found unequivocally on the Windows' top bar. It contains tools organized by Tabs with a gathering of buttons that assists you with dealing with records. The ribbon has the essential tabs, comprising the generally utilized orders; different tabs seem to be when you can utilize them.

A few buttons on the ribbon give decisions, while others send off an order. One essential advantage of the ribbon is consolidating those tasks or segment centers in a single spot that requires menus, task sheets, toolbars, and other UI parts to show. You additionally have one spot where you search for orders instead of looking through many spots.

Figure 2: The Ribbon Items

Ribbon Tabs and Components

The ribbon contains a movement of order tabs containing other orders. Access chief order tabs are Document, Home, Create, External Data, and Database Tools. What's more, every Tab contains social events of related orders, which surface a part of the extra new UI parts, for instance, the show, and one more kind of control that brings about choices.

The orders available on your ribbon similarly reflect the by-and-by unique article. For instance, if you have opened a table in Datasheet view and select the structure on Create tab in Structures pack, Access creates the Design considering the powerful table. That is, the name of your unique table is put in the new construction's Record source property. Furthermore, a number of ribbon tabs appear in unambiguous settings.

- **File**: File tab takes you to Backstage view with Open, Create, Save and more.

- **Home Tab:** Has frequently used commands. Create a different view, commands for text formatting, finding records, copying and pasting, rich text formatting to a memo, and more.

- **Create Tab:** Allows you to create and design Access elements like tables, forms, modules, queries, macros and reports.

Figure 3: The Create Tab

- **External Data:** This Tab provides commands that enable you to connect to other data sources. In this Tab, you can export or import data to/from file formats like Excel and CSV files (comma-separated values), databases like Access, SQL Server, Azure, ODBC data sources, and web services like SharePoint.

Figure 4: External Data Tab

- **Database Tools:** This Tab contains commands related to an Access database's inner workings. You get commands that enable you to compact & repair databases, create macros, create table relationships, analyze and tune your database performance, and move your database to different files like a backend Access database or a SharePoint server.

Figure 5: Database tools tab

- **The Backstage View**

Clicking **File** tab takes you to Backstage view. It offers menu options and commands to manage the current database and configure general Access settings. The Back button takes you back to the Access workspace.

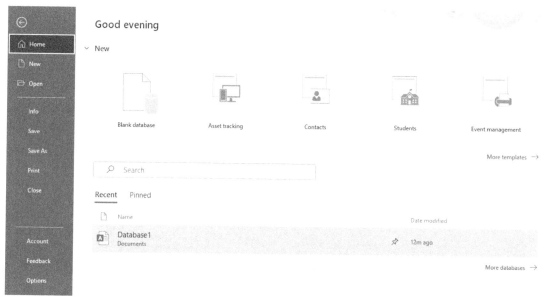

Figure 6: The Backstage View

An overview of the menu options in the Backstage view:

- **Info**: This option enables you to view and edit various properties of the current database, compact & repair the database, and encrypt the database with a password.

- **New**: This option enables you to create a new blank database or one from a predefined database template.

- **Open**: You can use this option to open your existing database, including viewing other recently opened databases.

- **Save**: This option takes you back to the Access workspace, where you can save individual Access objects.

- **Save As**: This menu option allows you to save or convert the current database. For instance, you may save the database with a different name, in which case, a copy of the database will be created. You can also convert the database to another Access format, as an object, or save it as a PDF or XPS file.

- **Print**: You can use this option to:
  - **Quick Print**: Directly forward the object to your default printer triggering any changes.
  - **Print**: Configure various printing options then print.
  - **Print Preview**: Gives you a preview of your document and allows you to change the pages you want to print.
- **Close**: Closes current database but leaves Access open.
- **Account**: View and manage information relating to the current Office user. Most of the options and settings here affect all Microsoft 365 applications installed on the computer, not just Access. For example, changing the Office Theme here will change it for all Office applications on the machine.
- **Options**: Launches the Access Options dialog box, which contains a series of settings you can use to customize Access, for example, language, display, proofing, the Ribbon, the Quick Access Toolbar, and other settings.
- **Feedback**: This allows you to provide feedback and suggestions to Microsoft and to explore the feedback from others.

2 LET'S START

CREATING A DATABASE TABLE

As I have said earlier, the most crucial part of constructing a database starts with table creation and entering data into the table. Kudos to Microsoft Access as it permits its user to create a database table with three different approaches, as I listed below:

- Creating database table from scratch.

- Creating a database table with the In-built template.

- Importing table from another database table.

CREATE A DATABASE TABLE FROM THE SCRATCH

It means you are creating a blank database table in which you will have to enter each field one after the other. Kindly open a database file and observe the itemized methods to create your database from scratch:

1. Tap **Create tab** and click on **Table Design** command to access the blank table.

Figure 7: The create table

2. The database blank table will come forth, giving you options to enter fields into your table.

Figure 8: The table design

CREATE A DATABASE TABLE WITH THE IN-BUILT TEMPLATE

A template makes database table creation easier. It involves little modification. Nevertheless, any user who wants to use a template in creating a database table must be proficient in Microsoft Access and know how to manipulate access gadgets. You have to pick one of the parts of the template in creating a database table, as you can see below:

1. **Contacts:** This is ideal for creating a database table related to contact addresses and phone numbers.

2. **Users:** it is the database that deals with email address storage.

3. **Tasks:** monitoring the project, such as the status and condition of the project.

4. **Issues:** it is concerned with a database table structured to deal with issues based on their importance.

When you create tables with templates, there are preformatted queries, forms, and reports you can attach to the tables. Observe the following steps in creating a database table with a template together with the preformatted forms, queries, and reports:

1. Kindly close all the **Open Objects** if any object is opened in the database working area when right-clicking any **open object title** and choosing **close All** on the drop-down list.

2. Once you close all the objects from the working area, tap on **Create** tab and click on the **Application Parts** menu.

3. Select template parts from the Application drop-down list under the QuickStart heading **(Contacts, Issues, Tasks, or Users).**

4. Create relationship dialog box will come forth asking you the pattern of relation you want. This warning will come if you have any other table in the database. Immediately you see the warning, kindly click "There is no relationship" and tap on **Create** Button.

5. The new table has been created with an in-built form, query, and report. You may have to click on design view at the status bar to view the table, field, and data type for any modification; modifying the template field name is another topic in this section.

IMPORTING A DATABASE TABLE FROM ANOTHER DATABASE TABLE

The easiest method to create a database table is importing from another. It gives you work-free effort in creating a database table, just like copying and pasting. To import a database table, ensure compliance with the following guidelines:

1. Tap on the **External Tab** and click on the **New Data Source** menu, then pick **From Database** menu on the drop-down list and lastly, pick **Access** from the fly-out list.

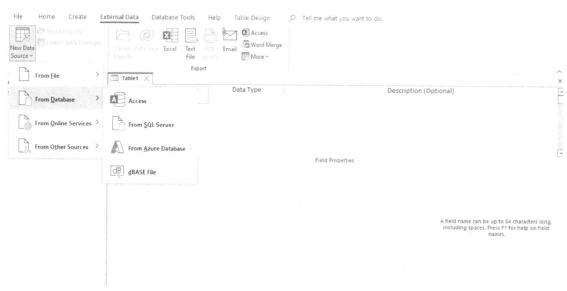

Figure 9: Importing a database

2. The Get External Data-Access Database dialog box will come forth, then Click **Browse** button to access File Open dialog box.

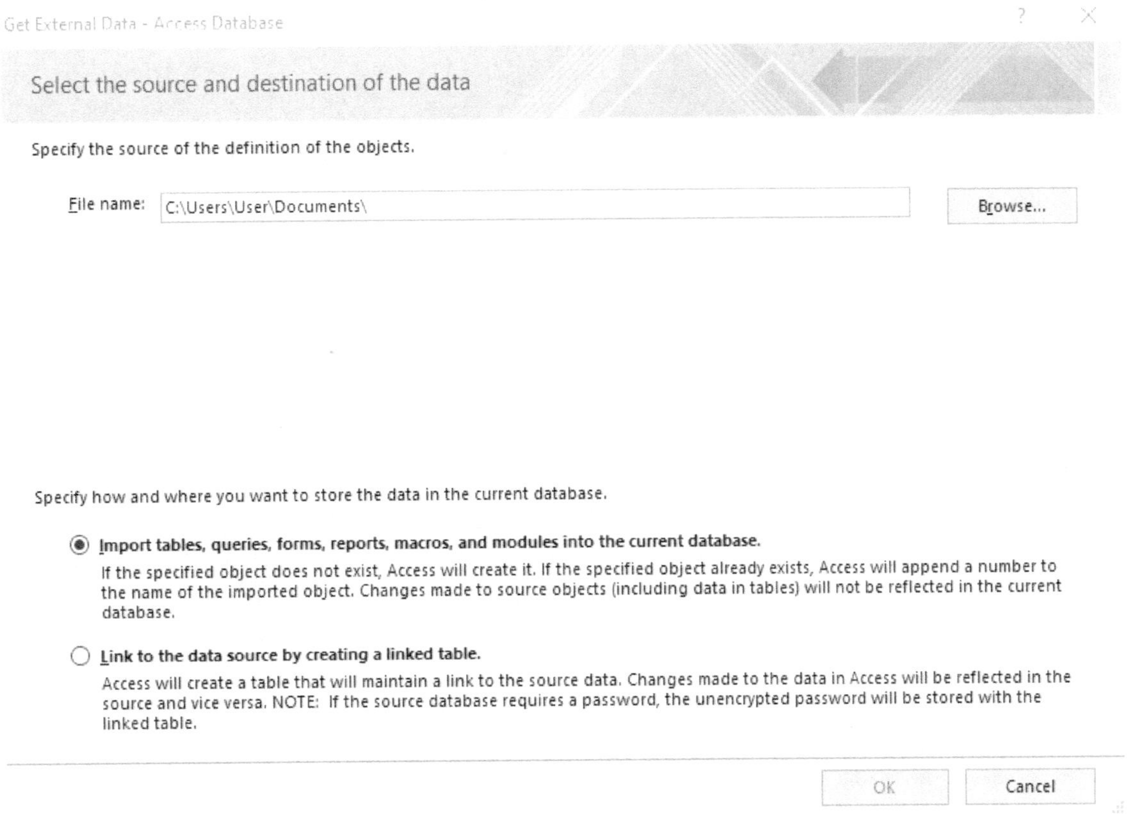

Figure 10: Importing an external database

3. Choose the **database file** with the database table you want and tap on the Open button to access Get External Data-Access Database dialog box.

4. Pick the first option with inscription(**Import Tables, Queries, Forms, Reports, Macros, and Modules into the Current Database**) and tap **Ok** to access dialog box for Import Objects.

5. Select the **database table(s)** you need with **Ctrl + click** for multiple selections under the Table tab (you have the option to "import table fields, format, and data" or "table fields and format only" by clicking on the Options button and select either Definition and Data or Definition only respectively under import tables.

6. Then click ok for authentication.

Note: you will be provided with a save import dialog box. Click on the close button. If your table to import has lookup fields, the imported table will automatically consist of lookup fields.

DATA TYPE	DESCRIPTION	SIZE
Short Text	It can be used to store all forms of Text that can't be used for calculation, such as addresses, telephone numbers, names, and so on	Ability to hold 255 characters.
Long Text	It is designed to store large forms of Text; only a few users use this type of data type	Ability to hold 63,999 characters.
Number	It is used for storing numerical data that can be used for calculation and currency computation.	Up to 16bytes
Large Number	It is used for storing very hefty data of numerical numbers for calculations and computations	Big Integer of about 450 bytes
Date/Time	It is used for storing date and time, and this can as well be used to determine the range of calculation	8bytes
Currency	It is used in storing monetary data for calculation	8bytes
Auto Number	It is used to store numbers in a particular sequence depending on how you set Auto Number, and you can assign it as the primary key provided there is no unique data in the database tables	4 bytes to 16 bytes
Yes/No	It is used to store logical values like yes/no, true/ false, etc.,	At most 8bytes

DATA TYPE	DESCRIPTION	SIZE
Attachment	It is used to store files, charts, and images. In addition, you can use it to attach files to the database table just the same way as attaching files to the email.	About 1GB
OLE object	It is used to insert database file links into another application file, such as a Word document	About 2GB
Hyperlink	It is used to store data that has a webpage format.	Maximum of 2048 characters
Calculated	It is used to store mathematical values from one field to the other.	Not much dependent on the data to be calculated
Lookup wizards	This is mainly used to create a drop-down list from which the worker can use to enter data in a way to eliminate the error of data entering	About 200 byte

How to export files from Access to Excel

- Select your table or database object you wish to export.
- Select "External Data" tab ribbon.

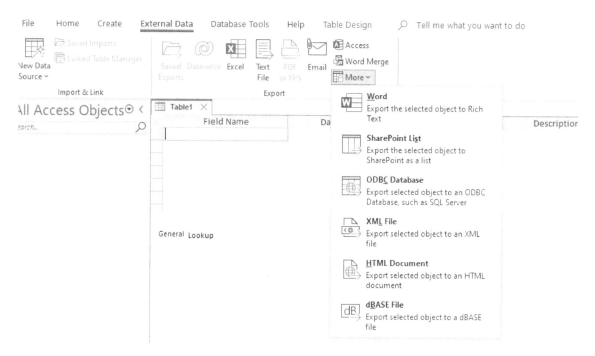

Figure 11: Exporting an item

- In Export group, select Excel. The wizard opens.

- Enter a name for the record (if you enter a comparable name as an ongoing activity manual in the goal, you will be incited to replace it), and snap on the Scrutinize button to pick a region for the report. Next, pick various decisions in the wizard, including planning, assuming you want to open the goal archive and export isolated or picked records. The record ought to be closed first on the off chance that you are replacing an ongoing activity manually.

- Select ok. Excel will consequently open if you have decided to open the objective document when complete. While naming the Excel workbook during this cycle, you might need to remember a date for the name if you want to hold duplicates of the information for precise dates. Toward the end of the cycle or when you return to Access, a dialog box will seem to inquire whether you need to save the export steps. If you are exporting consistently, you can save the Export ventures for reuse.

BUILDING DATABASE TABLES RELATIONSHIP

Table relationships indicate the connection between two selected database tables following the same information they have in them. The major means of creating the relationship is to use one table's primary key field against the other's foreign key fields.

Commit these two rules to memory any time you want to create a relationship between two tables:

- A relationship is only permitted within two related tables in the same database. For instance, the number field can't be compared with the text field with which they are unrelated. It must be a related field.
- Using Primary and foreign keys, you can tell Microsoft Access how the two tables will be related.

CATEGORIES OF RELATIONSHIPS

Database relationship is of three categories. Each category depends on the number of fields you want to relate with others in both tables. The following are the categories of database table relationship:

A One-To-Many Relationship

This is the most used relationship among the categories of tables relation. It is carried out by connecting one unique record (primary or indexed field key) field in one table against many records in other tables.

For example, consider a database for tracking orders with tables for customers and orders. A customer may place any number of orders. So, the user may reflect numerous orders in the Orders database for each customer represented in Customers table. Therefore, Customers table and Orders table are related one-to-many times.

To depict a one-to-many connection in your database architecture, add the primary key from the "one" side of the relationship to the "many" side of the relationship's table as an extra field(s).

In this case, you may, for example, add a new column to the Orders database called Customer ID, which is the ID field from the Customers table. Then, using the Client ID number in the Orders record, Access can locate the appropriate customer for each order.

A Many-To-Many Relationship

This establishes a relationship in both tables with more than two fields in each table; none of these fields is the primary field key.

Let's look at the connection between a product table and an Orders table. The user may include more than one product in a single order. Conversely, a single item may show up on numerous orders. As a result, each record in the Orders table may have multiple records in the Products database.

Furthermore, for each entry in the Products database, there may be many records in the Orders table. This is a many-to-many connection.

Because it breaks the many-to-many relationship into two one-to-many relationships, a third table, commonly known as a junction table, is necessary to represent a many-to-many relationship. The next step is adding the third table's primary key to each of your first two tables' primary keys. So, third table keeps track of each instance, or occurrence, of the relationship.

The One-To-One Relationship

Each record within first table can only have one matching record within your second table, and vice versa. Such kind of relationship is not very common.

A one-to-one connection can be used to segment a table with many fields, isolate a database area for security purposes, or store data specific to a subset of your main table. Both tables must include the same field if you locate such a relationship

You may create explicit table associations in the Relationships window or by dragging a field from the Field List pane. When using tables, Access searches for table connections to discover ways to link the tables. Before creating additional database objects like queries, forms, and reports, you should create table relationships for several reasons. Check them out:

- Table relationships help you construct effective queries.
- Your form and report designs should include table relationships.
- Table relationships enforce referential integrity, thus, avoiding orphan records. For instance, an order record referencing a different record but doesn't exist is

called an orphan record; an example would be an order record referencing a non-existent customer record.

- A primary key can be identified as a unique identifier assigned to each table when creating a database. Next, you assign foreign keys to associated tables using the primary keys as references. These primary key-foreign key references must remain in sync. Reference synchronization is supported by referential integrity that depends on your table relationships.

3 LET'S EXPLORE THIS IN DETAIL

Field Properties

Attributes describe the nature and behavior of data contributed to a field. More focus of a field is the data type that defines the nature of the data you can store there.

To set a field property, you must first locate the desired field's specific property on the tabs. The property you want to change is typically found under the "General" tab. The "Lookup" tab is only used when manually configuring "lookup" field attributes that display values from another table or list.

In the table's design view, you may modify the attributes of the custom table fields you create. When tables are opened in design view, the table design grid, which spans the top half of the screen, displays field names and data types. Below that, in the "Field Properties" section, on the two tabs labeled "General" and "Lookup," you can modify the properties of the field that is presently selected in the table design grid.

You can adjust the size, presentation, default values, and various other elements of the selected field by using the field properties on the "General" page. In the "Field Properties" section's right pane, you can hover the cursor on a property box to learn details about its use or purpose. You can Select the property box if you need further clarification on how to set the value of a specific property and then hit the "F1" key to get more help. A second window containing the help file will open, allowing you to read and print it as needed.

Field Size Property

- In a text field's "Field Size" property, you can specify the number you enter as the field's maximum character limit. In addition, the quantity of data that one can enter into the field can be limited. As the default field size, Access sets a text field's character limit at 255.

- Additional field characteristics can be added after a field is created and its data type is chosen. For example, you may customize field size to depend on the field's data type with extra features. For example, you may change the size of a Text field by modifying its Field Size attribute.

- When the "Field Size" is specified, number fields are distinct from text fields in that you select the type of numbers that the field can store before setting the field size. The possible sizes include "Byte," "Single," "Double," "Integer," "Long Integer," "Replication ID," and "Decimal."

- A long Integer is the standard field size for numbers. One of the most significant field sizes is this one. You can choose a smaller field size if you'd like because Access works better with smaller objects, so you can. If not, don't be concerned; you probably won't experience significant performance issues. Keep in mind that you should leave the setting at "Long Integer" if you are linking the "Number" column to an "AutoNumber" field in a table relationship.

- The Field Size property is particularly crucial for Number and Currency fields since it establishes the field values' range. For instance, a one-bit Number field can only store integers between 0 and 255.

- Each Number field value's required amount of disk space is likewise determined by the Field Size parameter. The number can utilize precisely 1, 2, 4, 8, 12, or 16 bytes, depending on the size of the field.

Note: The field value sizes for the Text and Memo fields are adjustable. Field Size determines how much space can hold a single value for various data types.

Field Caption Property

- When the Hyperlink Address or Hyperlink Sub-Address property is set for the control, the Text of the Caption property serves as the hyperlink display text for label or command button controls.

- The string expression for the Caption property has a maximum character count of 2,048.

- When dragging a field from your field list to create a control, the field's "Field Name" property setting is copied to control's Name property box. They will also reveal in label of the newly created control if you haven't provided a Caption property setting for your field

- The control's label caption or column header in the Datasheet view will be decided by the field's "Field Name" property setting if no caption is supplied. If the query field caption is left blank, the underlying table field caption will be used. Form1, for example, will be given a unique name by Microsoft Access if you don't define a caption for a button, form, or label.

- If you want an ampersand to appear in the caption text, enter two ampersands (&&) in the setting for a caption. For instance, enter Save && Exit in the Caption property box to display Save & Exit.

- Use the Caption attribute to attach an access key to a label or command button. The character you intend to use as an access key should be preceded by an ampersand (&) in the caption and usually underlined. Hit Alt and the underlined character to switch the attention to a control on a form.

Default Value Property

- You can set a field's default value, which will be applied to all new records. If necessary, you can modify the default value of a field when adding another entry.

- You can establish a default value by entering the desired value in the Field Properties' Default Value field. For example, the default text you enter for a Text field should be exemplified in quotes ("); for example, "Net 30." Likewise, date field values should be delimited by a number sign (#); for example, #1/15/95#. Access will naturally enter the number signs if you don't enter them.

- For instance, if a table has client names and addresses, and most of those locations are in Denver, you can determine Data as default value for State field.

The Express field's value can be changed only for the new record you make for an occupant client of Nairobi. A table's default value can't be changed after creation.

Required Field Property

- Use the needed attribute to specify whether a field must contain a value. If this attribute is set to Yes, all fields and controls associated to the field must contain a value; null values are prohibited.

- For instance, you could wish to confirm that each record's Last Name control contains a value. On the other hand, suppose you want to allow Null values in a field. Then, you must explicitly mention "validation rule Or Is Null" in the Validation Rule property setting and set required property to No.

Note that the required property does not cover AutoNumber fields.

Input Mask Property

- You can specify exactly the way data should be entered into your database using an input mask. It is an expression that details the formatting requirements for data when entered into the system.

- The format in which a phone number should be entered is specified below. Nine is optional, and the suffix "0" is required, implying that the area code is not compulsory here.

- An example of an input mask is given below:

(999) 000-0000

- Table fields, queries, forms, and report controls can all use input masks. The small dotted icon that looks like this can be Selected to start Input Mask Wizard:

Note that applying an input mask eliminates the need for using the wizard. You can enter the input mask straight into its cell if you know how to get it done. The only action taken by the input mask wizard is to create a suitable mask and insert it into the same cell.

Also, remember that you cannot apply an input mask to a field with a Date Picker on it.

Custom Input Mask

In line with the above discussion, you can create input masks in two ways:

Create using Input Mask Wizard (fastest way and easy).

The Input Mask Wizard's one limitation is that you may only use it to build input masks for fields containing ZIP codes, phone numbers, SSN, and timestamps.

By entering a string of characters in your Input Mask box, you can create the input mask on your own (the more difficult way). By looking at the table after this session, you can see what you need to enter to build an input mask if you wish to use this method.

FORMS

We have been manually inserting and entering data directly into our tables. Meanwhile, think of a situation where you need to have other individuals in your company add data to your table; it may not be as user-friendly to them as it is to you. The way out is to create a form making it pretty easy for other people in your organization to add data.

To **add a form**, firstly, select the desired table to create its Form by double-clicking on it.

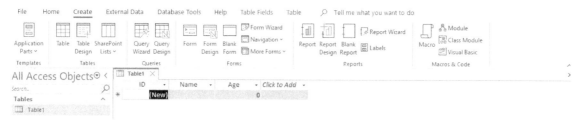

Figure 12: Creating a form

Now, click the **Create** tab and observe the **Forms** group. In the Forms group, we have different options to help you create a form.

However, clicking on **Form** is the easiest way to create a form.

Then, you are presented with a new form, and inside it is what your table looks like. Beneath the Form is the other table, which shows because we have linked the two tables together.

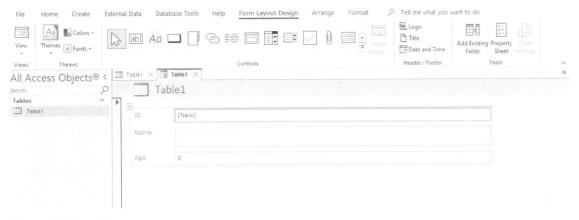

Figure 13: Form layout

You can use buttons at the Form's bottom to move from one Form to another and add a new (blank) record.

Customizing Forms

You can change the appearance of your Form by adding themes, colors, controls, logos, and more in the Design tab.

Design View

Just as we have Design View in tables, we also have Design View in forms. Click **Design View** button at the bottom right corner.

In the Design View, you can move different elements around and design the Form depending on how you want it to look.

Form View

The **Form View** button is at bottom right corner, which will allow you and other people to add records to your table. When you need to **add a new record** to your table through the Form, go to the lower part of your Form and click the **New (blank) record** icon. After clicking on it, you can fill out the Form and do the same for the linked table. After changing and customizing your Form, the next thing to do is save and close the Form. Then, click the **Save** icon to save and give it a name. Then, right-click your Form at the title bar and choose **Close**.

You should now notice a new category on your navigation panel, which says **Forms**. And in Forms, we have the Form we just created. You can double-click on it to open it.

4 REPORTS

This chapter will examine how you can create a basic report and add some features. Then, you'll see how to do some calculations in your reports and how you can do a specific report based on a query.

What is a Report?

A report is a way to organize or summarize the data so that it can be printed.

If you have a table with lots of data and have to print it just like that, it would be challenging to see all the data. It isn't very easy seeing it in that table format, especially if you're presenting that printed document to someone else. So instead, you can take that table and the data in that table or a query and base a report on it to make it look a little bit better.

The report is very similar to Forms, except you're just doing it in a printed format instead of a form.

Some Terminologies

At the top of a report, we put the **Labels** for the fields so that you know what each column is about, and then the section below contains the **Textboxes** that will contain the data from the table or the query that you are referring to.

You'll see a page header with labels that'll display as it is so that you can change those and it won't affect anything. However, the detail section has text boxes with the actual link to the fields in the table, so whatever is in the table will be displayed there. But, again, you can't change these because it will show the value for the fields.

You'll notice in your report that there are many blocks for each row in the design view. It only shows one, and it will just repeat this detail section again and again until it gets to the bottom of the page, and then it will recreate the page with a brand-new page header and then continue with those details.

Controls in Reports

You can add some controls to reports similar to what we did in forms. You can add a label, and if you want to specify other information on the report, you can use a label. You can use an image component if you connect to an image or show a little picture. If you wish to draw a line or separate something with a line, you can use the line component. You can use all these options, and we'll try them now in the report.

Creating A Report

Using our database from the previous examples, we're going to create a new report. To do that, click on **Create** and go to the **Report** options. You can design a report, have a blank report, add values, or use the **Report Wizard**. For this illustration, we are going with the last option.

After clicking on that option, you can specify the values you want in your report and the fields you want.

When you click **"Next,"** it'll ask if you want to do a grouping. We'll talk about grouping as we proceed.

Next, specify if you want to sort data by a particular field.

You can also select the layout for your report.

Lastly, you will be asked to give your report a name or title. Again, remember the naming conventions; since this is a report, you can use "Rep" as your prefix to know the difference between the table data and the report data.

Click on **"Finish,"** and it will show the Design and display the Form for you.

This opens up in the Print preview option, where you can see what each page will look like, and you can go straight to printing, but if you're not satisfied with the report, you can edit it to look better. To do this, go to the design view, and now you can change things over here.

If you notice that the birth date doesn't fit, you can change the report's layout, so look at the options at the top and work with those options.

If you see hashes on your report, you can't see the data in that field because it's not big enough. So to avoid that, you can rearrange some of these fields to make them spaced out and a little bigger.

If you want to make it justified or you want to make it left-aligned or right-aligned, you can do all those types of things by selecting Home and seeing all the options over here.

You can change the labels, and it won't affect the data but for the text boxes, leave them as is because that's going to fetch the data from the table and repeat this detail section.

You can also do other features to your report, such as adding another label at the top or editing a particular label. For example, let's say you want to put a line between each record. In that case, click on the Line icon under your Design tab at the top, which will put a nice line across. Then, you can right-click on that line, go to Properties, and see other options specific to that line. Please note that anything you do in detail will be repeated for each displayed record.

Calculations In Reports

Before we continue, you must know which control you may use to enter these formulas, and that control is the Text box. When designing your report, you may include a text box and then enter the formula within the text box. You cannot use standard Text in a text box; if you wish to enter standard Text, use a label.

So, what are the types of calculations that you can use?

If you want to add up all the values in a particular field, then you will use Equals sum (=**SUM**), and then in brackets, you will write down the name of the field that you want to do the summing on. This is very similar to Excel, except that instead of cell references like A1 to A10, you'll write the field name you are referring to. You'll notice that the field name is in square brackets; that's the format. If you do not have spaces in your field names, then you can write them just as is, and they will put the square brackets in for you but if you have spaces, use a square bracket. Another is the "**MAX,**" which finds the biggest value out of that particular field. Then, there's the "**MIN,**" the smallest value. And then there's the "**AVG**" if you want to find the average amount paid.

There's also a "**COUNT**" where you can count how many records there are so that you can count all the emails, for example, but because you're counting all the records, you don't need to specify a particular field. Instead, you could use a *****.

The first four functions can only be used with numerical fields or fields that have numbers. For instance, it is possible to find average amount paid or the sum of all the outstanding amounts, so for anything that has to do with currency or numerical value, you can use those first. **Conversely, COUNT can be used in any field, so when you use the COUNT, you can use any field in it or** a *****.

Please note that these functions cannot be used in the header or footer of a page. This is because you can't find the sum of all the values on a particular page or some or the max of all the values on a particular page. So these will not work in the page header and footer, so don't put them there.

If you wish to include a formula in the page header or footer, you may use the current page number. To do this, say = **[PAGE]** keyword, which will give you the current page number. If you want the total number of pages, that'll be = **[PAGES]**.

If you want to use the NOW field, which is =**NOW ()**, that will give you the current date and the time, and then you can format that to display just the time or the date.

So, let's go to the report we designed earlier. Right-click on it, and go to the design view so you can change the details of your report. You'll notice that by default, it's already added a couple of options like "**Now**" and that of the pages.

Let's say you want to find the average of everything in the report. Ideally, you put that in the report footer. But first, click on the text box, which will give you a label and a text box. For example, to find the sum of all the "Paid," that will be written as =**SUM(Paid)**.

Notice that there are no square brackets because you typed just as it is. However, it will put the square brackets in for you. Remember to give it a label as well.

You could also put it in the report header, but that's not a great place to keep in mind that we put all our formulas in the report footer.

Next, go to view; in this case, use Report view, and when you scroll down towards the bottom where you have report footer, you can see that the total amount paid is now included.

If you need to make changes, go back to your design view, **right-click**, and go to Properties. For example, you can change it to currency or add decimals to make it look better.

Remember to always put in the correct spelling, and you can't put the title in a text box. You can only do that in a label because you want the Text to be displayed as it is. This is a basic calculation that you can perform on your reports. To gain full mastery, you can practice with the other formulas.

5 QUESTIONS AND ANSWERS

How do you query a Database?

A database query solicits information from a database, the item program that stays aware of data. A query response regularly returns data from various tables inside your database. You can query to recover some data or alter information in your database, for instance, adding or dispensing with data Users can pick how to use that information reasonably when they get a query response. The real job of a database query is to recuperate information from a database for the user. A database query has several other vital functions, including

- Compiling information
- Presenting results clearly
- Filtering data
- Adding criteria

The two standard sorts of database queries are select queries and action queries.

Benefits of using a Query

- Use verbalizations as fields.
- View records that meet the models that you decide on.
- Accumulate information from a couple of information sources. A table ordinarily shows information that it stores.
- View information just from fields you have more interest to preview. Once a table is opened, you can see each field. A question is a useful strategy for saving a determination of fields.

Creating Basic Queries

To create a Simple Query, follow the procedure below:

On the create tab, identify the Query Wizard.

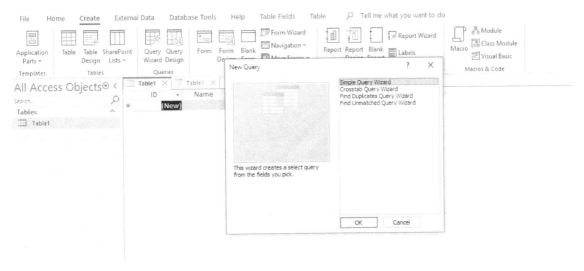

Figure 14: The query wizard

Click Ok.

Addition of field allows you to add up to 255 fields from multiple table or queries.

For each of the fields:

- Under the Available Fields, select your field for easier addition to Selected Fields list. Next, use the double right arrows (>>) to move the field.

- Under Tables/Queries, select table or query containinf the specified field.

- Then click next.

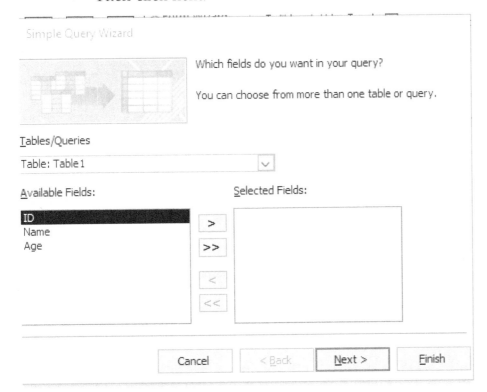

Figure 15: Addition of fields

The wizard will inquire whether you believe the question should return subtleties outline information.

Select Summary, and then choose Summary or detailed option Options depending on the user.

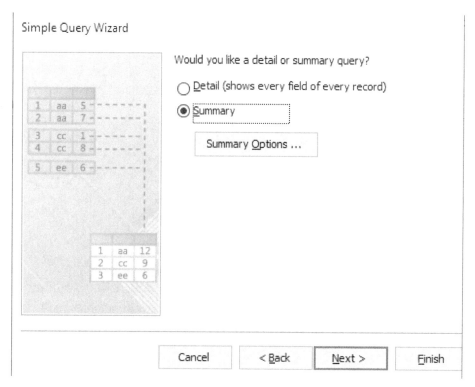

Figure 16: Choosing summary

Show the fields that need a summary and define ways of maintaining that data in summarized form in the dialog box.

You may choose the following for each of you number field:

- **Max:** Query will bring the most significant value within your field.

- **Avg:** Results to average of your values.

- **Sum:** Sums up the values.

- **Min:** Brings the smallest value.

Pick the proper Include records in the database name check box.

Select OK. You may provide a title to the query, decide if you should open or alter your query and the click Finish.

- **Working with "AND" and "OR" conditions**

An AND operator allows a query to match two conditions, for instance, which people are entrepreneurs and have a vehicle.

An OR operator allows a query to match only a rare example of the situation, for instance, what people go to the office or work from Home.

Sorting and Filtering Data in Queries

Access empowers you to work with huge data measures; sorting and filtering let you change how you coordinate and see your data, making it more beneficial to work with, which suggests it will generally be trying to learn anything about your database by just checking it out.

Sorting and filtering are devices that permit you to coordinate your data. Filtering data permits you to hide insignificant data and spotlight the data you're enthused about. At the point when you sort data, you are dealing with it.

Sorting Data

Records are put legitimately after being sorted with data assembled. Accordingly, sorted data is regularly simpler to scrutinize and comprehend than unsorted data. Access sorts records by their ID numbers. In any case, there are various elective ways the client can sort records. For example, the client could sort the data in a database having a spot with a baked good shop in different ways:

- Clients could be sorted by name, city, or postal division where they dwell.

- The client could sort orders by request date/time or by the username of the clients who presented the solicitations.

- You can sort Text and numbers in two ways: in rising and dropping requests. Rising means going up, so a climbing sort will coordinate numbers from humblest to generally critical and Text from beginning to end.

- Things could be sorted by name, classification (like pies, cakes, and cupcakes), or cost.

To Sort Records:

Choose a field you need to sort.

Choose the Sort & Filter group on the home tab.

Selecting either Ascending or Descending button.

To save the sorted group, select the save option.

After you save the sort, the records will stay sorted until you play another sort or wipe out the continuous one. To wipe out a sort, select the Remove Sort order. **Filtering Data** Filters permit you to see just the data you need to see. When you make a filter, you set standards for the data you need to show. The filter then, at that point, look through each of the records in the table, track down the ones that meet your hunt measures, and briefly conceals those that don't.

Filters are valuable since they permit you to focus on detailed records without being diverted by the data you're uninterested in. For example, assuming you had a database that included client and request information, you could make a filter to show clients living inside a specific city or orders containing a particular item. Seeing this data with a filter would be more helpful than looking for it in an enormous table.

To apply a filter:

Select the drop-down arrow close to the field you want to filter.

A drop-down menu with a checklist will appear and deselect everything the option needed to filter.

Select OK.

Toggling your filter permits you to turn it on and off. To see the records without the filter, Select the Toggle Filter order. To re-establish the filter, select it once more.

Creating Filter from a Selection

Filtering by determination licenses you to pick itemized data from your table and find data that is relative or not the slightest bit like it. Making a filter with a choice can be more beneficial than setting up a good filter on the off chance that the field you're working with contains various things. Assuming you were working with a confectionary store database and expected to search for all things whose names contained the word chocolate, you could pick that word in one thing name and make a filter with that determination. For instance,

- Does Not End With consolidates regardless of records from those whose data for the picked field closes with the pursuit term.

- Does Not Contain involve regardless of records from those with cells containing the picked data?

- Closes With consolidates simply records whose data for the picked field closes with the inquiry term.

- Contains consolidates records with cells that contain the picked data.

6 THE BEST ACCESS PLUGINS

If you're looking for a better way to customize your Microsoft Access applications, you may want to look into UI Builder. This product offers a wide variety of features that nearly every Access user can benefit from. It allows you to focus on your primary needs while offering powerful features that would otherwise be time-consuming to create. It's also user-friendly and includes powerful features experienced software contractors and developers need.

Access SQL Editor is an add-in for Microsoft Access that enables you to save SQL with syntax highlighting and formatting. It also has features such as regex search-and-replace and automatic code formatting. You can also find and replace objects and design time properties in any Access form.

Total Access Analyzer is another excellent Access plugin for improving database performance. It analyzes database objects, detects 280 errors, and applies Best Practices. It can also create right-click menus, reveal database object dependencies, and create modern dialogs. Total Access Detective is available in free and paid versions, so you can try it out without paying a single penny.

MS Access is one of the most popular DBMSs used by small and medium-sized businesses and private individuals. Because it's user-friendly and doesn't require extensive programming skills, it's ideal for beginners and those with little experience in database management. However, you should know that other DBMSs work similarly; some are free.

7 TIPS, TRICKS & FAQ WITH COMMON PROBLEMS AND SOLUTIONS

Whether you're developing a business or personal database, finding a solution for a common problem with Microsoft Access is possible. Some solutions can solve these issues, from data entry errors to broken database links. In addition, Microsoft Access has many useful features that make it easier to work with the data. For instance, you can create a search field to find records in one or more of the tables. Once you've created a query, it is possible to save it for future use. Alternatively, you can choose to view the values of database fields.

Learning how to use Microsoft Access can be difficult. This program has many features, and it can seem overwhelming. However, there are plenty of tips and tricks for Microsoft Access that can make your life easier. Let's take a look at some of them. Using these tips, you'll maximize productivity and make the most out of the software.

When you use the program, keep a current backup of your data before making any changes. When using the program, you may accidentally delete a field. Then, Access will remove that record from the table. If this happens, it won't let you undo your changes.

Another tip is to hide the ribbon. Many people hate the ribbon in Access, but hiding it isn't that difficult. You can do it with a few easy steps. First, double-click a tab to minimize its visibility, and Access will remember that you don't want the ribbon to open. Another easy tip for minimizing disk space is choosing the data type optimized for the data. This will save on storage space and processing time. Selecting the smallest data type is best, but you can also use secondary indexes with a large table. These secondary indexes provide performance gains of an order of magnitude.

DO AWAY WITH DATA MISMATCH

Data mismatch means entering data into a field different from the data type you specify for the field or having different data types between primary and foreign key that connect the two tables you put into the relationship. Data mismatch prevents you from establishing a relationship between the table you put to the relation window or query design window, affecting your query result.

WRONG CRITERIA BRING WRONG OR NO QUERY RESULT

Make all necessary efforts to enter the correct criteria into each field you put to the grid field, and do not make the mistake of entering criteria into the wrong field. These two mistakes are the consequences of wrong or no query results.

THERE SHOULD BE A LINK BETWEEN THE TABLES IN THE RELATIONSHIP

It is of great importance for the tables in relationship to have a direct link, which means there should be "implement referential integrity" between the tables in terms of recorded data and the data type in them.

EACH TABLE SHOULD HAVE A PRIMARY KEY, AND IT SHOULD BE A NUMERIC DATA TYPE

It is the principle of the database table to have a primary key that should uniquely identify other data in the field to make the relationship between tables convenient. However, it is not about having a primary key field only. The field should be a numeric data type to make that uniqueness an easy task, such as AutoNumber, ID, which should be numeric, and so on. On the other hand, using no numeric data type renders the uniqueness of the primary key field meaningless such as city name, first name, etc.

VALIDATING ACCESS DATA TYPE

The simplest and easiest way to restrict wrong data into the database table is to program the data type with validation field properties. This command issues a warning error anytime there is an attempt to enter data different from the programming data through the validation rule in the field properties.

Encrypting an Access Database

In earlier MS Access versions (before 2007), it was possible to create user accounts with different permissions to different sets of objects, which was called multi-user security. That feature is no longer available in the .accdb versions (2007 and later). In the current version of Access, each user will use the same Password to access the database in a multi-user environment.

Be careful when encrypting and always remember the password. You can't decrypt the database without your Password. Hence, it would help if you were careful when creating a password for your database. You don't want a situation where you cannot access important data because the Password has been lost. For that reason, only set a password if necessary for your working circumstances.

To encrypt an Access database with a password, follow the steps below:

Step 1: Open your database in the Exclusive mode.

1. Open Access.
2. Access opens to the Backstage view.

   Note: If you already have another database open, click the **File** tab to display the Backstage view.
3. In the Backstage view, click **Open > Browse**.
4. In **Open** dialog box, navigate to database you wish opened and choose the file.
5. Click drop-down arrow near **Open** button and select **Open Exclusive** from the pop-up menu.

Step 2: Encrypt the Database with a password.

1. With the database now open in Exclusive mode, click **File** tab to return to Backstage view and select **Info > Encrypt with Password**.

Access displays **Set Database Password** dialog box.

2. In the **Password** box, enter your desired password. Repeat in **Verify** box to confirm it clicking **OK.**
3. Click **OK** at the next prompt to encrypt the database with a password.
4. Close and then reopen.

Access will display **Password Required** dialog box.

5. Enter your Password, and click **OK**.

Access will decrypt and open the database.

Important: You mustn't forget your Password. To be on the safe side, before you protect your database with a password, ensure you've written down the Password and stored it in a safe place where it can be retrieved if necessary. Unfortunately, Microsoft does not provide any methods to access a password-protected Access file where the Password has been lost.

8 THE STRATEGIC SHORTCUTS

SHORTCUTS FOR ENTERING DATA IN DATASHEET VIEW

KEYBOARD SHORTCUTS	DESTINATION
↓	Moving to next record of the same field
↑	Moving to previous record of the same field
Enter or Tab or right arrow	Moving to next field in the same record.
Shift + Tab or right arrow	Moving to previous field in the same record.
Home	Moving to first field of current record.
End	Moving to last field of the current record.
Ctrl + Home	Moving to first field in the first record.
Ctrl + End	Moving to last field in the last record.
Page up	Moving up one screen.
Page down	Moving down one screen.

GENERAL SHORTCUTS

KEYBOARD SHORTCUTS	PURPOSES
Ctrl + O	Open an existing database
F11	Show/ hide navigation pane
F2	Switch between edit mode navigation mode in the datasheet and Design view
F1	Open the Help window
Ctrl + F1	Expand/collapse the ribbon
Ctrl + S	Save the database objects

KEYBOARD SHORTCUTS	PURPOSES
Ctrl + X	Move selected content to clipboard
Ctrl + C	Copy selected content to clipboard
Ctrl + V	Paste clipboard content to selected cells or sections.
Ctrl + F	Open Find in find and replace dialog box in both views
Ctrl + H	Open Replace in find and replace dialog box in both views.

GRID PANE SHORTCUTS

KEYBOARD SHORTCUTS	PURPOSES
Arrow keys, Tab, shift + tab keys	To move among cells
Ctrl + Spacebar	To select an entire grid column
F2	To switch between edit mode and navigation mode
Ctrl + X	Move selected content to clipboard
Ctrl + C	Copy selected content to clipboard
Ctrl + V	Paste clipboard content into the selected cells or sections.
Ctrl + Home	Moving to first field in the first record.
Ctrl + End	Moving to last field in the last record.

9 CONCLUSION

Can you now see the efficacy of Access? Access is here to help you more than Excel or Word can do for you, Access main focus is to fill up the weakness of Excel by managing large arrays of data. Managing large arrays of data involves entering unlimited data, querying the data, and then using the query result to generate a professional report for the user. This is the best option for whosoever wishes to learn Access, does not know where and how to get started, or you have little experience but wish to dig deeper to know more about Access. This book is ideal for all levels of users, including those who have learned Excel before. However, your Excel experience is not enough until you know how to match your Excel work hand in hand with Access.

This manual user guide is adequately prepared to expose you to the mystery that guides the management of databases and to put you on the easy track for learning the use of Access in creating a perfect database. Happy exploration.

Printed in France by Amazon
Brétigny-sur-Orge, FR

11976952R00027